# THE RULE

# THE RULE

## ST. JOHN PAUL II'S RULE
*for a*
## JOY-FILLED MARRIAGE
*of* DIVINE LOVE

*Theresa and Peter Martin*

 WOJTYŁA INSTITUTE PRESS
— for the joy of truth —

NIHIL OBSTAT:      Very Rev. Samuel A. Martin
*Censor Librorum*
December 14, 2022

IMPRIMATUR:     ✠ Most Rev. William Patrick Callahan
Bishop of La Crosse
January 12, 2023

 WOJTYŁA INSTITUTE PRESS
— for the joy of truth —

Published in the United States by Wojtyła Institute Press, an imprint of the Wojtyła Community & Institute, Inc., Wisconsin.

www.wojtylaci.com

 LIBRERIA EDITRICE VATICANA

Texts of Karol Wojtyła/St. John Paul II © *Libreria Editrice Vaticana,* published with permission.
Polish texts translated by A. Pata, 2020.

Cover image: photo of the original, handwritten Rule by Cardinal Karol Wojtyła. © Archdiocese of Kraków, printed with permission.

Cover graphic design: Christina Ghioto, littleloretto.com

ISBN 978-0-578-39565-4

PRINTED IN THE UNITED STATES OF AMERICA.

First Edition, 2023.

## WE DEDICATE THIS BOOK TO

Our dear savior Jesus Christ, "Oh Fount of life, unfathomable Divine Mercy, envelop the whole world and empty yourself out upon us." We place all we do in your merciful hands; Jesus, we trust in you!

Our dearest Mother Mary, we cry out in a loud voice, *Totus tuus, Maria!*

St. John Paul II.

His Eminence, Raymond Leo Cardinal BURKE.

Professor & Mrs. Stanisław and Ludmiła Grygiel.

Fr. Przemysław Kwiatkowski.

The WCI Board of Directors and Leadership Council, with a special thanks to chief editor, Mrs. Emily Lofy for her keen eye and selfless heart.

To our parents, Phil and Liz Slattery and +Mark and Barbara Martin, for their witness of marriage and the years of selfless love they gave (and continue to give) to all their children and grandchildren *(and great grandchildren!)*.

To our children: Gregory, Louis, Leonardo, Emmanuel, Damian, Anthony, Marie-Thérèse, Charles, and our babies in Heaven. You are our light, our joy, and our way to holiness. We love you.

# CONTENTS

FOREWORD                                                iii

INTRODUCTION                                             xi


## PART ONE

## The Rule That Leads to Joy

1   IN SEARCH OF LASTING JOY                              3

2   GENESIS OF THE RULE: THE COMMUNITY
    *ŚRODOWISKO*                                         17

3   THE IMPORTANCE OF *HUMANAE VITAE*                    23

4   A CLOSER LOOK AT THE RULE                            31

5   "THE RULE FOR MARRIED COUPLE GROUPS
    *HUMANAE VITAE* (PREMISES)"
    – BY CARDINAL KAROL WOJTYŁA                          39

6   THE RULE IN ACTION                                   43


## PART TWO

## Going Deeper

7   INTRODUCTION TO THE TWO
    ACCOMPANYING TEXTS                                   55

8   "REFLECTIONS ON MARRIAGE" – BY FR. KAROL
    WOJTYŁA
    *SYNOPSIS*                                           59

ORIGINAL TEXT                                          60

UNPACKING THE TEXT                                     76

9  "LOVE IS THE MORAL FOUNDATION OF
   MARRIAGE" – BY BISHOP KAROL WOJTYŁA

   SYNOPSIS                                            87

   ORIGINAL TEXT                                       89

   UNPACKING THE TEXT                                  100

10 COMMUNITY AND COMMITMENT                            111

11 THE REAL AND THE IDEAL: *THE CULTURE OF THE
   PERSON*                                             121

12 *HUMANAE VITAE*                                     135

13 CHRISTIAN MORALITY: *ENCOUNTER WITH
   CHRIST*                                             147

14 MARRIAGE UNITY AND CONJUGAL SPIRITUALITY            155

15 STUDYING MARRIAGE, APOSTOLATE, AND PRAYER           173

16 LIGHTING UP THE DARKNESS *WITH THE SPARK OF
   POLAND*                                             191


   WOJTYŁA COMMUNITY & INSTITUTE                       201

   ABOUT THE AUTHORS                                   203


   APPENDIX

   HISTORY OF CHURCH'S TEACHING                        205

   LEARN MORE ON *HUMANAE VITAE*                       211

# FOREWORD

When Pope Saint John Paul II gave the task of developing the Pontifical John Paul II Institute for Studies on Marriage and Family to the then Father Carlo Caffarra, a young professor of moral theology, Father Caffarra encountered seemingly insurmountable difficulties. As a result, he wrote to Sister Lucia dos Santos, one of the three shepherd children to whom the Virgin Mother of God appeared at Fatima from May to October of 1917, to ask for her prayers. The now Servant of God responded with the promise of prayers, observing that in the present time the most vicious attack of Satan upon man would be directed against marriage and the family. The late Cardinal Caffarra, whose friendship greatly blessed me, frequently recounted the contents of the letter which he received from Sister Lucia. Although he had received the letter some 40 years earlier, he observed how the truth it announced continues to be ever more verified in our time.

Satan whom Our Lord himself taught us is "a murderer from the beginning" and "the father of lies"[1] has indeed found his most insidious and effective act of hatred for man in convincing man to rebel against the good order of marriage and family life as established by God the Father at the Creation and as restored and fortified with Divine Grace by the

---

[1] Jn 8, 44.

Redemptive Incarnation of God the Son. Rebelling against God, man today denies his or her very nature as male and female, and the irreplaceable mission of the love of man and woman in marriage as the cradle of new human life through procreation, through cooperation with God the sole Author of Life. The rebellion becomes ever more outrageous as, for example, small children are taught that they can decide their sexual identity, instead of receiving it as a gift from God, and are subjected to the worst kind of abuse in trying to change the identity which God, in His unceasing and immeasurable love, gave them at their conception.

In such a situation, the only response can be a return to God, to God the Son Incarnate Who teaches us the truth about human life and its cradle in the love of a man and a woman in marriage. He chose to be born into the family of the Virgin Mary and her True and Virgin Spouse Saint Joseph and to grow up as their Son[2] in the home they had formed by their marriage. He worked His first miracle on behalf of the newlyweds at Cana.[3] With great courage, He made clear that His Redemptive Incarnation restores the original order which God gave to marriage at the Creation.[4] In short, inviting us to give our hearts to His glorious-pierced Heart, He pours forth into our hearts divine life and love without cease and without measure, enabling us both to understand our true

---

[2] Cf. Lk 2, 52.
[3] Cf. Jn 2, 1-12.
[4] Cf. Mt 19, 3-12.

nature and to live in accord with it, finding the joy and peace which we so deeply desire.

Pope Saint John Paul II, as a young priest and Bishop, understood that, even as Satan's attack today is upon marriage and the family, so, too, the way of victory over the lies and death he sows far and wide is through safeguarding and promoting marriage and the family, according to God's plan, according to the teaching of Christ in His holy Church. As a priest and Bishop, as a living instrument of Christ's pastoral charity, he directed himself, first and foremost, to couples and to the families which they formed through the grace of Holy Matrimony. During his years as Bishop, he assisted marriages, eventually developing what is called *The Rule* for married couples, after the publication of the Encyclical Letter of Pope Saint Paul VI, *Humanae Vitae*.

During the first four years of his pontificate, he devoted his Wednesday Audience Addresses, one of the principal means of teaching of the Holy Father, to marriage and the family. The first session of the Synod of Bishops, during his pontificate, was devoted to the family. His Post-synodal Apostolic Exhortation, *Familiaris Consortio*, made available to all the faithful and to all persons of good will the fruit of that Apostolic meeting. His writing on marriage and the family, above all, *Familiaris Consortio*, merits our renewed and deeper study as we continue to safeguard and promote human life and love.

Theresa and Peter Martin, drawing upon their extensive study of theology and upon the grace of their marriage in Christ, have accepted the mission of bringing *The Rule* of Pope Saint John Paul II to the English-speaking public. What is more, their mission includes the foundation of a nonprofit organization which provides support, resources and practical tools to spouses who desire to live *The Rule*. With the publication of the present volume, *The Rule* and two other important texts of the saintly Pontiff become available for the first time to the anglophone world.

The book makes *The Rule* and other texts accessible to as many readers as possible. Thus, it is divided into two parts. The first part is simpler and more straightforward, presenting *The Rule*, providing historical background and situating *The Rule* within the context of contemporary culture. The second is more theological, using the other two documents to expound upon the meaning of the various points set forth in *The Rule*. While the second part is deeper in its presentation, Theresa and Peter Martin offer many personal examples from their own our life as husband and wife, father and mother, and from the lives of other married couples. In doing so, they illustrate the critical connection of sound theology to everyday Christian living.

At its core, *The Rule* helps couples to live the truth set forth in the truly prophetic Encyclical Letter of Pope Saint Paul VI, *Humanae Vitae*. It is directed to building up the spiritual life of the couple, which has, as its form, conjugal love, that is, it helps the couple to develop their relationship with the Divine Family of the Most Holy Trinity, which is the model of their conjugal relationship in the family. In short, it helps them to respond ever more faithfully and generously to the grace of the Sacrament of Holy Matrimony. *Humanae Vitae* courageously addresses the truth to contemporary culture. The truth is that God, and not man – as contemporary culture maintains – is the author of human life and sexuality. Following *The Rule*, a couple grows in the gift of conjugal love received on their wedding day and becomes a wellspring of grace for their neighbors and for society, in general. All couples who study and follow *The Rule*, no matter what may be the stage of the development of their love for another, will grow ever more perfectly in the image of the pure and selfless love of the Most Holy Trinity.

The Wojtyła Community & Institute (WCI) is the nonprofit organization which Theresa and Peter Martin have founded to fulfill more perfectly their mission of spreading knowledge and practice of *The Rule* of Pope Saint John Paul II. The Mission Statement of WCI reads: "Trusting the Rule of St. John Paul II, we are a family of families, striving for holiness, strengthening marriages, and living the truth of *Humanae Vitae* with JOY!"

WCI (Wojtylaci.com) is prepared to assist in the starting of a Married Couple Group by which couples mutually support and strengthen each other in conjugal love, according to the divinely-inspired wisdom of Saint Paul: "Bear one another's burdens, and so fulfil the law of Christ."[5] WCI has workbooks and other resources for a Married Couple Group as it seeks to know *The Rule* and to apply it to everyday life.

---

[5] Gal 6, 2.

These resources become the means to develop a deeper conjugal spirituality.

As Pope Saint John Paul II understood so well, living conjugal love in a totally secularized culture requires heroism in those who are called to practice conjugal love. Recognizing the challenge to living conjugal love in our time, the saintly Roman Pontiff understood the irreplaceable service of the community and, in particular, of the community of married couples.

As a priest and Bishop, he gathered couples into community with each other, into a "family of families." *The Rule* provides the guide for the forming of many such communities of couples to assist each couple to live in accord with God's plan for them as it is handed on to them in the Church's constant moral teaching. Through prayer, commitment, and community, the six points of *The Rule* help married couples remain strong in faith and its fruit, joy, while meeting the struggles and sufferings inherent in taking up daily the cross with Christ, in following Him daily in the way of pure and selfless love.[6] They help married couples to go frequently to the font of divine love which makes them capable of heroic love for each other, no matter how weak they may have been or may be.

The family formed by marriage is the first cell of the life of society and of the Church. In the Church, the family is called the *Ecclesia Domestica*, the Church in the home. As Pope Saint John Paul II frequently reminded us, the strength of society and of the Church depends

---

[6] Cf. Mt 16, 24; Mk 8, 34; and Lk 9, 23.

upon the strength of the family. The publication of *The Rule* of Pope Saint John Paul II and the foundation of the Wojtyła Community & Institute offer great hope for stronger and healthier families and, therefore, for the strength and health of life in society and in the Church.

It is my hope that the publication of *The Rule* and the service of the WCI will inspire and strengthen married couples to live more faithfully and deeply the mystery of conjugal love as God has intended it from the beginning and for which Christ never ceases to pour out from His glorious-pierced Heart the grace of pure and selfless love into the hearts of husbands and wives. Couples whose hearts rest in the Sacred Heart of Jesus will indeed be a font of light in a world which has grown very dark, a font of joy and peace in a world marked by so much despair and violence.

The great beauty of *The Rule* of Pope Saint John Paul II for married couples is the knowledge of the grace they have received through the Sacrament of Holy Matrimony. Such knowledge, so securely grounded in the truth, inspires couples to live daily and heroically the mystery of conjugal love as a blessing to them and to the whole world. May each of us who come to know *The Rule* be faithful and courageous in spreading its message to all whom we meet!

In the name of all who will read and study the present volume, I offer heartfelt thanks to Theresa and Peter Martin for the publication of *The Rule* in English and for the work of the WCI in assisting couples to follow it. May God bless them and their family.

May God bless you and your home! Through the intercession of Pope Saint John Paul II, may you witness ever more heroically to the mystery of conjugal love, and may Holy Matrimony be ever more known, safeguarded, and promoted in the Church and in the world.

Raymond Leo Cardinal BURKE

7 October 2022 – Feast of Our Lady of the Holy Rosary.

# INTRODUCTION

This book has been a labor of love. It began with research for a dissertation then developed into a vocation. The translated texts in this book are from a newly rediscovered collection of St. John Paul II's documents from his time in Poland when he was a priest then Bishop Karol Wojtyła. The main text: "The Rule for Married Couple Groups *Humanae Vitae* (premises)"[7] by Cardinal Wojtyła is a simple, six-point rule that he wrote after the proclamation of *Humanae Vitae* and as a way for married couples to live out this teaching with "full understanding and full love."[8] The other two texts, written around the same time, help to illuminate the meaning of The Rule.

We want this to be accessible to all readers; even if you have never picked up a theology book, *this is written for you*. What St. John Paul II has given us in The Rule is what we need in our troubled times. It is a way forward for couples to do more than continually persevere in their faith but to truly live with divine

---

[7] K. WOJTYŁA, "Reguła dla grupy małżeństw *Humanae vitae* (założenia)", in AWDR M 23. (AWDR – an official abbreviation of the Archives of the Office of the Metropolitan Curia of Krakow for family and pastoral care – *Archiwum Wydziału Duszpasterstwa Rodzin Kurii Metropolitalnej w Krakowie*). Translated by A. Pata, 2020.
[8] *The Rule*, point 4.

love and experience lasting joy! We have broken the book into two parts:

*PART ONE: THE RULE THAT LEADS TO JOY* shares the love and joy we seek, how The Rule helps us get there, and the need for this in our society. *PART TWO: GOING DEEPER* allows readers to delve into what St. John Paul II meant by the different facets of The Rule so they can better understand his vision for the Married Couple Groups. This second part can be read sequentially or used as a reference guide.

St. John Paul II's writing is rich and profound, and we did not want you to miss this wisdom; however, we know that sometimes all that's needed are quick facts. This is why *PART ONE* was created—to give everyone easy, full access to The Rule with the key to crossing a threshold of lasting joy.

In order to create and support Married Couple Groups according to The Rule of St. John Paul II, the Wojtyła Community & Institute was created on the fifty-second anniversary of the promulgation of *Humanae Vitae* on July 25, 2020. We will share more about this in later chapters, but you can also learn more, by visiting wojtylaci.com. We look forward to hearing from you!

We humbly remain God's servants, knowing it is not our merit, but His great love that gave us the opportunity to share such a gift with you.

*All for His glory,*
*In the hearts of Jesus and Mary,*

*Theresa and Peter Martin*

PART ONE

# THE RULE THAT LEADS TO JOY

# 1

## IN SEARCH OF LASTING JOY

*"Take this ring, as a sign of my love and fidelity. In the name of the Father, and of the Son, and of the Holy Spirit..."*

This is a book about love; more exactly, it is about the love that knows no end, the love our hearts yearn for. The love that consumes, that reverberates, that heightens—it is a love that costs everything—yet offers everything. It is a love that transforms us from broken, fallen creatures into the children of God we were meant to be. It is about Love. The One who made all, who is all, and who brings everything back into Himself. It is the calling of the Spirit and the passion of the Bridegroom wrapping around us and carrying us forth to the heart of the Father in eternal glory. It is Love that never fails. Love that comforts, that caresses, that sweetens every sorrow. Jesus Christ is the Love for which we ache in the depth of our souls; the Love that we crave at the heart of every desire we feel. It is Love that penetrates our realities, our despair, our messiness, our daily stress, our heartbreaks, our faults, our mistakes, and, yes, our sins. And this Love, He doesn't cover over it. He doesn't suppress us but renews all things. Love doesn't blot out our individuality; Love perfects it! Love enters into every fiber of our being and remakes us so that we're born again into His divine life. We walk on the earth, but we live in Heaven, and we find great and lasting joy. Love can change everything, but only if we are open to His grace.

When spouses slide the wedding rings on each other's fingers and vow in the sight of God to be faithful and true, they are inviting God's love into their marriage. They are opening their hearts to the grace of the sacrament of marriage. At that moment of commitment, a new bond is formed, not only between husband and wife but also with God. This precious relationship between God and the spouses together is their conjugal spirituality.[9] The newlyweds are caught in a swirl of blessing and emotion; in this extraordinary moment of divine Love reaching down to join two imperfect people, their hearts are open...and Love enters in, and there is joy.

So, what happens? How do we so often lose our joy? Even though every marriage begins with joyful hope, somewhere, somehow, it can become subdued. The wedding music fades, the honeymoon ends, and the demands of life begin swirling around the spouses again. This new, extraordinary married life soon is

---

[9] We will see later on how St. John Paul II explains conjugal spirituality, this unique relationship of the union of spouses with God.

absorbed into the ordinary of daily activities. The busyness, the stress, and the pace of the world around them begins to crowd in. The tidal wave of secularism within culture pushes against them. Even as they strive to live their lives faithfully, it takes all their effort to hold their ground and not be pushed backward. And after the drudgery of daily tasks, the daily effort, the daily pursuit and struggle, it seems that real, lasting joy is like the horizon. No matter how hard you try to arrive at it, it is always just out of reach.

Our modern world is fast-paced and frenzied, but other cultures throughout the centuries had their own challenges. Nevertheless, the saints found joy. What are we missing? Have you ever read the lives of the saints and thought, *I wish my faith brought me that kind of joy*. The joy that led others to nickname St. Philip Neri the "laughing saint" even while he endured slander from without and within the Church. The joy that gave St. Teresa of Avila such an intimate friendship with God that she was able to tease Him out loud after she fell off her carriage into the mud, "If this is how you treat your friends, no wonder you have so few of them!" The joy that gave St. Lawrence the cheerfulness to say, while he was being burnt alive, "Turn me over. I'm done on this side!"[10] The joy that enlivened the hearts of the early Christians so they could go to their deaths in the arena of devouring beasts singing songs of praise to God.

---

[10] Incidentally, did you know he is the patron Saint of comedians and chefs?

Yet, how often do we whine when our Wi-Fi is slow? This is not an accusation as much as a confession. Far too frequently, we become anxious about many things—situations like the next crisis in the world or what our future will be. Perhaps during these times we forget Who created the world in the first place. Who set the earth on its path. Who put the stars in place. Who sent His only Son for the salvation of us all? Even as we pursue our faith, frequent the sacraments, open our hearts to God, something about this culture is so taxing, so exhausting. Practicing our faith can feel burdensome and challenging, which can leave us feeling lost, alone, and isolated.

It may be that we feel exhausted because we are pushing back against a tidal wave of secularism in our culture as well as against an increasingly anti-Christian ideology. As much as we strive for holiness, at times it seems the most you can do is just hold your ground and pray you don't fall backward. As the world continues to ridicule, alienate, and tempt us with a so-called "easier" way, it is understandable why some couples may find the battle discouraging.

We have seen the outcomes of this discouragement, and the results themselves can create further dismay. Many couples fall out of practice of the faith or choose to disregard certain teachings because they determine them to be just "too difficult" or claim they are "out of touch" or "archaic." Other couples push forward in faith with a white-knuckled, sheer force of will. Neither way produces lasting joy in their lives. What are we missing? *There must be another way.*

# St. John Paul II's Rule

St. John Paul II was a man of love. Originally from Poland, he was the pope from 1978 to 2005. In his first encyclical he emphasized man's need for love — to encounter He who is Love: "Man cannot live without love. He remains a being that is incomprehensible for himself, his life is senseless, if love is not revealed to him, if he does not encounter love, if he does not experience it and make it his own, if he does not participate intimately in it."[11] He saw the love between spouses as a reflection and extension of God's divine love. Where others of his era considered marriage as a lesser order of life, seeing it as what you did when you did not have a religious vocation, St. John Paul II saw something more. He saw in marriage a real vocation, a true calling from God. He saw the gift that couples could offer: to be a living witness of God's love to the world. When people can see God's love, they have hope. A world without divine love is desperate and bleak. Spouses have great potential for holiness precisely because they find themselves joined in love. When living out their marriage connected to God, married couples can reflect the life-giving love of God to the world.

St. John Paul II witnessed a culture shifting much like our own; he saw an increasingly anti-Christian sentiment rising around him. He saw young people

---

[11] St. John Paul II. *Redemptor Hominis*, 1979, n. 10.

beginning to be influenced and disheartened by the culture. He knew we needed another way. He took the opportunity to offer a way to help spouses get beyond the struggle and enter more deeply into divine love so that they might live with lasting joy.

When St. John Paul II was a priest in Poland, he said that in an increasingly anti-Christian culture, living an authentically Christian marriage "does demand an increased effort toward reaching and preserving the moral perfection than ever before."[12] If the culture is not on our side, then we will have to work extra hard to live an authentically Christian marriage. Our commitment to pursue holiness must be even stronger than marriages of generations past. No wonder we feel exhausted.

He said being Christian in a secular culture requires a certain "heroism." We need to live with *heroic virtue*. This is not easy. We need to know that. We need to be committed. Living out a truly Christian marriage today takes great courage. But with God all things are possible (Mt 19:26). It can be done, but we must ask how. How do spouses find the moral stamina to live heroically and stand up to the onslaught of secularism? How do we find the strength to persevere? How do we go beyond the white-knuckled faith and find lasting joy? St. John Paul II gives us the answer in The Rule.

---

[12] *Reflections on Marriage, section 3. Economy and Personalism*

St. John Paul II wrote *The Rule for Married Couple Groups* when he was Cardinal Wojtyła.[13] He wrote The Rule after St. Paul VI's encyclical *Humanae Vitae* was promulgated. *Humanae Vitae* was written to address the particular issue of the use of contraception in marriage. When St. Paul VI wrote that "each and every marriage act must remain open to the transmission of life," he was merely affirming teaching that was well established within the Church dating back to the first century.[14]

Even though *Humanae Vitae* was written to address this specific concern, St. John Paul II saw within it the central aspect of spousal love. He said *Humanae Vitae* gives us the conditions that will safeguard self-giving, authentic love and will preserve the essence of spousal love from being falsified.[15] In other words, the truth about spousal love made explicit in *Humanae Vitae* is the key to living true love, a love that resides in the heart of the Father and a love that produces lasting joy.

The Rule is a way for married couples to actualize or *make real in their marriages* the teaching of *Humanae Vitae*. In doing so, they will unlock lasting joy. Couples

---

[13] K. WOJTYŁA, "Reguła dla grupy małżeństw *Humanae vitae* (założenia)", in AWDR M 23. (AWDR – an official abbreviation of the Archives of the Office of the Metropolitan Curia of Krakow for family and pastoral care – *Archiwum Wydziału Duszpasterstwa Rodzin Kurii Metropolitalnej w Krakowie*). Translated by A. Pata, 2020.

[14] For more on *Humanae Vitae*, see part 2: Going Deeper, chapter 5 and in the appendix is a list of quotes from history to confirm this statement.

[15] Stephen Milne, *Love and Fruitfulness: Marriage and family in the teaching of the Church*, (Maryvale Institute: Birmingham, 2014), 65.

need to understand not just why this teaching is true, but how to apply this truth joyfully to their lives. The difficulty was (and still is) that with a culture so ardently opposed to such a teaching as *Humanae Vitae*, the "why" of it had to be clarified and explained. With each new generation increasingly exposed to the errors of modern society, this continues to be necessary. Unfortunately, the "why" has often overshadowed the "how."

This seems to be a missing piece: How does a couple move from understanding the truth to living the truth in their lives with joy? Once we understand why *Humanae Vitae* contains the truth of spousal love, we see the importance and the challenge of learning how.

The exciting news is that The Rule gives us this how. The heart of The Rule emphasizes living according to the norms of Christian morality and cultivating a deep, unifying spirituality in our marriages. As we begin to unpack this, it is important to remember that the Christian life is not simply an intellectual acceptance or a following of a list of rules.[16] It is a continual conversion of our hearts toward Christ, with the help of grace.

---

[16] Servais Pinckaers, O.P., *The Sources of Christian Ethics*, (Catholic University of America Press: Washington, D.C., 1995) 115-125. Fr. Servais Pinckaers, O.P. is a renowned ethicist who studied under the same Dominican theological influences at the *Angelicum* in Rome as then Fr. Wojtyła.

# Continual Conversion in Love

When people first find out that St. John Paul II wrote a six-point rule for married couples, they may envision an easier path. We're accustomed in our age to be promised the easy way: five tips to increase muscle mass, for example, or ways to become smarter in ten minutes a day following a specific plan. This is not the way of our Lord. Remember the rich young man? He is the perfect example of our human weakness of wanting the easy way: "What must I do..." He probably was so excited when Christ reaffirmed what he had already been doing: following the Ten Commandments, fasting, tithing, and so on. Yet, we all know that man walked away sad. Why? Because God does not want our actions; He wants our whole lives! He knows that we will not be happy until we respond to the Love that our hearts long for. We will not be truly joyful until we have given ourselves to Love! St. John Paul II knew that too, which is again why he wrote, "He remains a being that is incomprehensible."[17]

We have all heard that God's ways are not our ways (Is 55:8-9). The way in which He leads us to Himself often can be puzzling. We desire holiness; this is indeed our goal, but the pursuit of holiness needs to look different than striving for goals in other areas of our lives. Have you ever had a goal to reach in work, academics, or health? We pursue it; we power through it; we work hard. We do all the tasks we need to do.

---

[17] *Redemptor Hominis*, n. 10.

We put forth all the effort and hope, in the end, that we will be successful. When we approach our spiritual lives, we oftentimes slip into that same way of operating. Have I said my prayers? Check. Have I attended Mass? Check. Have I gone to confession, taught my children about God, said the Rosary, studied the Catechism, and asked questions about what I didn't understand? Check, check, check, and...hmmm...maybe check. If we did all the right things, we are good and God loves us now, right? Not necessarily.

All these actions are good and holy, and the pursuit of living a holy life is praiseworthy (and necessary). Yet, we must realize: there is nothing you can *do* to make God love you. God loves you right now — with infinite abundance! Even if you never did any of those things, He still loves you. He doesn't just tolerate you until you get your life in order. He loves you with a passionate, vibrant love even when you sin. His love is not conditional. He loves you because of who He is, not because of what you've done. You don't need to be perfect before you approach God; God wants to meet you right where you are. He wants to be the one to heal your wounds, kiss away your tears, rid you of sin. He wants to come into that daily mess and fill it with His divine, merciful love.

It's almost upside down from the way we are accustomed to achieving goals. Our ultimate goal — life with God — is at our doorstep. The goal is right before you. And He will help you on your spiritual journey, imbuing each of those holy actions with more of His grace. Instead of it being first a list of tasks to achieve then finally reaching the goal at the end, our Goal is already with us. We must walk in the path of His love and do the actions that help us open our hearts more and more to His grace and merciful love.

Your holiness is not found merely in the actions; rather, it is found in the way you allow God to meet you in those actions and in the way you allow each moment of grace to affect your heart. We continue to do what is right while realizing that we already have a relationship with a loving God.

The title of St. John Paul II's text, The Rule, can also conjure similar ideas of tasks that need to be completed or rules that need to be followed — *or else*. Three strikes and you're out. The good news is that this couldn't be further from the truth, especially regarding The Rule. It is a guideline, true, and it does have points to follow; however, everything is undertaken in order to affect and deepen the spouses' conjugal spirituality — their relationship with God. The Rule points the way to open ourselves and our marriages to be more receptive to God's merciful love. It guides us gently in love, and we find ourselves nestled in the heart of the Father.

Christian faith is an encounter with a Person: Jesus Christ (Jn 14:6). Christ "is not just a teacher of morality… He is the embodiment of what He teaches and therefore the source of the life we are called to live."[18] And when we choose to follow the teachings of Christ, we grow in unity with Him.[19]

Living our faith is more than agreeing to and following a rulebook. It is allowing *He who is Truth* to permeate every aspect of our lives, so that we may reflect His life in us more and more. This continual conversion of our lives to Christ and His way must penetrate beyond simple actions and resonate in our hearts.

# Be Courageous

God is waiting for us to let Him into our hearts more deeply. But we still constantly have to combat the busy and chaotic society around us. We need to be honest with ourselves and recognize that we may be more influenced by the culture than we realize. George Weigel, historian and renown biographer of St. John Paul II, describes how this culture affects us. He calls this busyness of the world the "totalitarianism of stimuli," which pulls us away from who we are meant to be and reduces us to mere reactions: of this or that comfort. This sort of addiction to the comfortable becomes like a dictator in our lives and keeps us from

---

[18] John Saward, *Christ is the Answer*, (Alba House: New York, 1995) 94.
[19] Pinckaers, 115-125.

becoming our best selves, who God made us to be.[20] For example, when we catch ourselves whining when our Wi-Fi is slow, that might point that we put too much of an emphasis on comfort. We don't need to beat ourselves up about it, but now that we can recognize it, we can more easily detach ourselves from whatever it is and not allow it to steal our joy. We must all courageously look at where we may be influenced by the world that surrounds us. When we allow Christ to peel back this influence, we detach from these little comforts and can become who we are meant to be.

This brings us back to the excitement of The Rule. St. John Paul II gives us the perfect gift that answers the question of how we can joyfully live out the truths of our faith on marriage so that God's divine love can permeate everything we do. Through The Rule (and two accompanying texts), St. John Paul II guides married couples to a joy-filled marriage that can only be found through divine love.

---

[20] George Weigel, *Wojtyła's Walk Among Philosophers*, accessed via http://eppc.org/publications/Wojtyłas-walk-among-philosophers/.

# 2

# GENESIS OF THE RULE:
## *THE COMMUNITY ŚRODOWISKO*

Did you know that St. John Paul II was a part of a Catholic community? It was called *Środowisko* (pronounced: shrō-dō-vīskō, which translates loosely to *environment* or *ambiance.*).[21] This was not a

---

[21] To understand the *Środowisko* community and experience, three main sources will be referenced. The first is the definitive biography of St. John Paul II, *Witness to Hope*, which is rich in extensive explanations of all angles of the political, social, and religious influences throughout Fr. Wojtyła's life. [George Weigel, *Witness to Hope: The Biography of John Paul II*, (HarperCollins Publishers: New York, 1999).] In addition, its sequel, *The End and the Beginning*, an essential piece of the total biography of St. John Paul II was studied. [George Weigel, *The End and the Beginning: Pope John Paul II – The Victory of Freedom, the Last Years, the Legacy*, (Doubleday: New York, 2010).] The third is an Italian text: *Bellezza e spiritualità dell'amore coniugale*, which translates as *The Beauty and Spirituality of Conjugal Love*. [Ludmiła Grygiel, Grygiel, Stanisław and Kwiatkowski, Przemysław, *Bellezza e spiritualità dell'amore coniugale: Con un inedito di Karol Wojtyła*, (Cantagalli: Siena, 2009).] Two of the three authors were members of the *Środowisko* group and, therefore, have keen insight into the experience firsthand, which they share in the book.

formalized community, but a "rich tapestry" of a network of friends that centered around their faith.[22] The *Środowisko* community began as a small group that formed while Fr. Wojtyła was a pastor at St. Florian parish and a chaplain to university students in Kraków.

When it started, this group was comprised of university students, and they first called themselves *Rodzinka* (pronounced: rōd-jīnkǎ), which means *little family*. It began on the feast of the Presentation of the Child Jesus, when students gathered with a "'young, poorly dressed, pious priest' who turned out to be in charge of the parish's chaplaincy to students." [23] Fr. Wojtyła encouraged the students to start a choir, taught them Gregorian chant, and invited them to Mass on Wednesday morning. This Wednesday morning Mass became a staple of the growing group.

If we think the world is chaotic now, imagine living in communist Poland. It was a difficult time to be Catholic. The Communist leaders did not allow priests to associate with the laity outside the Church and forbade most Catholic associations. Every time they gathered, they had to be creative and courageous. The Wednesday morning Mass and philosophy study conferences on Thursday evenings began to build a strong community of students. Despite the dangers, the charisma and love of their priest kept all the students coming back. The group of students—around twenty at this time—was not an exclusive clique. The

[22] Weigel, *The End and the Beginning*, 42.
[23] Weigel, *Witness to Hope*, 98.

students went out into the community and began acts of mercy, visiting and caring for the sick and needy in their area.[24] Fr. Wojtyła was active in the lives of the students. As their pastor, he went on excursions with them, offered days of reflection for them, and offered Masses on their patron saint's feast days. They often met in people's homes and went mountain climbing, skiing, kayaking, and camping together.

Fr. Wojtyła received the title *"Wujek"* (**vū**-yĕk, which means *uncle*) from the group in 1952 because it was not safe to call him *Father* in public. It was a life-giving environment for the students and such a drastic contrast to the emptiness and dullness of the communist regime. "As yet another member of *Środowisko* put it, 'We could live more freely because we were free inside.'"[25] Through *Środowisko*, Fr. Wojtyła taught the students how to live the way of the Gospels.

When Fr. Wojtyła was removed formally from his pastoral post in the parish to finish another doctoral degree, he was still a pastor to his *Środowisko* community. As time moved on, so did their lives. Many students married and Fr. Wojtyła was there to guide them, often giving days of prayer and reflection for each couple.[26] For *Wujek*, love was "the truth at the center of the human condition, and love always meant self-giving, not self-assertion."[27] As he says in a letter

---

[24] *Ibid.*
[25] *Ibid.*, 100.
[26] *Ibid.*, 101.
[27] *Ibid.*

to one of the members, Teresa Heydel, in 1956:

> Everyone ... lives, above all, for love. The
> ability to love authentically, not great
> intellectual capacity, constitutes the
> deepest part of a personality. It is no
> accident that the greatest commandment
> is to love. Authentic love leads us outside
> ourselves to affirming others: devoting
> oneself to the cause of man, to people,
> and, above all, to God.[28]

When the couples began having children, Wojtyła
was there to baptize and celebrate with the families. He
did not just celebrate the sacrament of baptism; but
went to their homes and invested in their lives. "'He
always had time,' Teresa Malecka recalled. 'He
understood that to baptize means to come home, to be
with the family, to bless the baby sleeping in the bed.
We didn't have to ask him to do this; he wanted to do
it.'"[29] This was a priest who lived fully the self-giving
love that he encouraged the married couples to live. He
did not shy away from conversations about human
sexuality either, teaching "his young couples that the
sexual expression of their love within the bond of
marriage was a beautiful thing, a holy thing, even an
image of God."[30] Young Fr. Wojtyła lived his priestly
vocation in self-giving love long before ever writing
papal documents about the idea of it.

---

[28] *Ibid.*
[29] *Ibid.*
[30] *Ibid.*

## *Communio Amicorum* to *Communio Sanctorum*

*Środowisko* was a community of people learning how to live out their faith together, even in the midst of a communist regime. A married couple part of this group, Ludmiła and Stanisław Grygiel, recalled that Fr. Wojtyła lead the youth's pastoral care with a strong and intense friendship. He taught them, and at the same time was learning together with them *"to be the Church,* to receive and give of themselves."[31] This gift of themselves was not merely a theory; it was visible in all they did. Fr. Wojtyła lived out his love for others through the gift of himself within life's daily challenges. Because of this, his life and the laity who followed him were directed toward holiness and the love of God.[32] They learned how to be the Church and "(i)n the Church, the *communio amicorum* (community or *communion* of friends) helps people realize their vocation to holiness, and from this comes the *communio sanctorum* (the communion of saints)."[33]

His *Środowisko* would remain friends with him even after he became pope. At his funeral Mass, "several dozen members of Karol Wojtyła's *Środowisko*" could be seen. They "had flown in from Kraków the day before, stayed in parks overnight, and were still in their

---

[31] Grygiel, 70.
[32] *Ibid.*
[33] Grygiel, 65.

outdoor    apparel    (which    seemed    entirely
appropriate)."[34]

It was because of and for the married couples of this
vibrant community that Cardinal Wojtyła wrote The
Rule. The Rule would be the path that will help lead
couples from a *communio amicorum* to *communio
sanctorum*, which is why The Rule was written not only
for individual couples but for Married Couple Groups.
It is only through the strength and the support of a
Christian community that spouses can rise above the
struggle, live heroically virtuous lives and find lasting
joy! When you have the support of friends, you can do
things you otherwise not feel you have the strength to
accomplish.

By following The Rule written by St. John Paul II,
spouses will have a path to guide them toward
holiness. As they support other couples (and are
supported by an intentional, faithful community), they
will find their love purified in divine love and cross the
threshold to lasting joy in their marriage, becoming the
shift of culture they've been longing for.

---

[34] Weigel, *The End and the Beginning*, 392.

# 3

# THE IMPORTANCE OF *HUMANAE VITAE*

We mentioned earlier that The Rule was written right after the promulgation of St. Paul VI's encyclical, *Humanae Vitae*. St. John Paul II wrote The Rule to help married couples understand and live the truth of *Humanae Vitae*, which is the core of every teaching of marriage. This prophetic document emphasizes the fact that God, and not man, is the author of love, life, and human sexuality. In an article he wrote around the same time as The Rule, St. John Paul II affirmed that *Humanae Vitae* gives us the conditions that will safeguard self-giving, authentic love and will preserve the essence of authentic spousal love from falsification.[35]

If we seek to follow The Rule our Holy Father left for us and hope to find divine love and joy through it, we must take a deeper look at *Humanae Vitae*. For Cardinal Wojtyła, The Rule did not just help couples by giving them a set of regulations to follow. He saw The Rule as supporting couples so that their *conjugal*

---

[35] Milne, 65.

*spirituality* would grow and transform their lives. The purpose of The Rule, he says, is to build our conjugal spirituality to actualize (or make real) in our marriages the teachings of the Catholic Church on marriage, especially *Humanae Vitae*. Conjugal spirituality is a spiritual reality that penetrates all of who the husband and wife are. It is "the living relationship with the Trinity and with the spouse, in the actualization of the total delivering up of Christ for the church."[36] The truth of spousal love explained within *Humanae Vitae* is the core of understanding the spouses' united relationship with the Blessed Trinity (conjugal spirituality). If, as St. John Paul II says, *Humanae Vitae* gives us the conditions which will safeguard self-giving, authentic love from being false,[37] then, if we wish to grow our conjugal spirituality, we can only do so if it is "a truly and integrally honest love."[38]

Through *Humanae Vitae*, St. Paul VI reminds us that everything must be seen in light of man's final destiny and that love must be human, total, faithful, and fruitful.[39] He also affirms each act "must remain open to the transmission of life."[40] In following Vatican II, which claimed the criteria for discerning judgements about the transmission of life must be objective, Paul VI proclaims that "it is not licit, even for the gravest

---

[36] Grygiel, 21, "attualizzazione della consegna totale di Cristo per la Chiesa."
[37] Milne, 65.
[38] *Ibid.*, 16.
[39] *HV*, 9.
[40] *Ibid.*, 11.

reasons, to do evil so that good might follow."[41] In the rejection of contraception, he promotes the practices of natural family planning (NFP) that work with the woman's natural fertility cycle and build self-mastery.

St. John Paul II further explains this "total-ness" of spousal love. Every one of us, as a human person, has a certain quality because a person is one who is in relation.[42] This is a reflection of the personhood of the trinitarian nature of God. Each Person of the Trinity is understood as in relation to another. We say "God the Father," but what is father except one who has a child? How do we understand "God the Son" except by one who has a parent? Each Divine Person is understood by this 'in relation' character. So, too, we as human persons, and made in the image and likeness of God, are made to be in relation with another.

Whenever one gives a gift of oneself to another, they fulfill their own personhood and become more clearly the image and likeness of God. In marriage, this total gift of self to another must include their fertility. To separate unitive and procreative, St. John Paul II explained, is to divide the unity of a person, which is contrary to Christian view. This division is Cartesian, and enforces the idea that only the mind matters (and the body does not), and utilitarian, which says that the body can be used but does not really matter. St. Paul VI saw with great clarity how contraception would

---

[41] *Ibid.*, 14.

[42] Cardinal Karol Wojtyła, "The Anthropological Vision of *Humanae Vitae*," January 16 (L'Osservatore Romano: Rome, 1969), 3.

lower the human person by diminishing his value. It would make a man/woman more of a commodity to be bought and sold for pleasure and less of the person of great dignity, which he was created to be.

St. John Paul II gave such a beautiful and tangible affirmation of *Humanae Vitae* within his diocese with the writing of The Rule, but this came at a time when the political climate was extremely volatile. Did you know that there was an intense adverse reaction to *Humanae Vitae*? What we are going to describe is the culture in 1968. Our world has become increasingly more secularized and anti-Christian since then.

Antigovernment protests and the sexual revolution were rising into full swing, which was creating a secularist culture already in upheaval, even before *Humanae Vitae* was proclaimed. To give a taste of this environment, George Weigel, in his biography of John Paul II *Witness to Hope*, describes: "(t)he timing of *Humanae Vitae* could not have been worse; 1968, a year of revolutionary enthusiasms, was not the moment for calm, measured reflection on anything. It is doubtful whether any reiteration of the classic Catholic position on marital chastity, no matter how persuasively argued, could have been heard in such circumstances."[43] What made St. Paul VI's task even more challenging were the leaked documents from the commission that he had established.

From this commission, there were two opinions. The so-called "Majority Report" rejected the natural

---

[43] Weigel, *Witness to Hope*, 210.

law arguments used in the past, specifically those found in the papal document *Casti Connubii*, and used a "totality" argument instead to support the use of contraception.[44] This totality argument states that "it is not necessary for each marital act to remain open to procreation so long as the 'totality' of the acts are so open."[45] (*If you apply this idea of totality to other promises of marriage, you can see its error; for example, when considering faithfulness, under this totality argument, adultery would be allowed, for not all sexual acts have to be faithful in marriage as long as the "totality" of the acts are faithful.*) St. Paul VI would reject the arguments of the

---

[44] "With the opening of the Second Vatican Council Pope John XXIII convened a small commission to advise him on these questions (of the contraceptive pill). After John's death, Pope Paul VI greatly expanded what was called the Commission for the Study of Problems of Population, Family, and Birthrate until eventually it grew to approximately 60 members, including three married couples ... Karol Wojtyła was a member of this commission but was unable to attend meetings ... Private documents of the commission were leaked to the press, individuals abandoned lifelong support of the Church's teaching on contraception, and, in general, the existence and momentum of the commission led many to believe that Paul VI would come to find some sort of contraception compatible with the Catholic view of marriage ... The majority of the commission had voted in favor of a change in Church teaching ... They wrote two reports known as the Majority Report and the Majority Rebuttal ... The Minority Report, on the other hand, stressed the constancy of Church teaching on contraception and argued that a change would be disastrous for Church authority." Janet Smith, *Why Humanae Vitae was Right: a Reader*, (Ignatius Press: San Francisco, 1993), 503-506. For further understanding of the Majority Report, see also: The Majority Report: "The Question is Not Closed" in *The Birth Control Debate*, ed. Robert Hoyt (The National Catholic Reporter: Kansas City, MO, 1968).
[45] Smith, *Why Humanae Vitae was Right: a Reader*, 505-506.

Majority Report but not before its circulation set up the false expectation that the Pope would proclaim the acceptance of contraception. This was the complicated stage set before St. Paul VI.

As soon as *Humanae Vitae* was published, criticism and misinterpretations of it flooded academia. One of the most notable was Fr. Charles Curran, then a professor at the Catholic University of America, who held a press conference within 24 hours of the promulgation and announced to all faithful that he had a list of more than 80 theologians who disagreed with this document and that people did not have to follow it but instead should rely on their own conscience. His document was called the "Theologians' Statement" and was signed by more than 600 theologians.[46]

Although some attempt to regain control of the dissenters occurred, especially towards the priests who refused to teach *Humanae Vitae*, the American Catholic hierarchy was mostly silent. Dr. Janet Smith recounts that some who were in the seminary in the 1970s recall being told not even to read *Humanae Vitae* but to read Fr. Curran's statement instead.[47] The Congregation of the Doctrine of the Faith attempted to counteract the growing misinterpretations that stemmed from an incorrect reading of the documents

[46] Smith, *Why Humanae Vitae was Right: a Reader*, 507-501. *Also Cf.*, Daniel Callahan, *The Catholic Case of Contracpetion,* (The Macmillian Company: New York, 1969), 67.
[47] Janet Smith, *Humanae Vitae 50 Years Later: History of Dissent and Defense,* (Augustine Institute: Greenwood Vllage, CO, 2018).

of Vatican II; but with the number of dissenters growing, it was a challenging time for the Church.

Fifty-some years later, we live in a culture that is more hostile to the teaching of *Humanae Vitae* than it has ever been. We hope this short history affirms the necessity of The Rule. The heart of the teaching of truth on marriage and family is found in *Humanae Vitae*. And remember what St. John Paul II said: living out the truth of marriage in our time demands an even higher level of morality.[48] We must be courageous. And we need the support of other couples to stand strong despite the negative culture boxing us in. We must not back down from this teaching but rise up with greater fervor to defend it and, more importantly, to live it.

---

[48] *Ibid*. Emphasis added.

# 4

## A Closer Look at The Rule

You may be thinking, as we did, "Wait, St. John Paul II wrote The Rule for Married Couple Groups? How come I have never heard of this?" The main reason you haven't heard of it is because it has never been published into English until now. When St. John Paul II first wrote it, The Rule didn't take off in Poland. It was later archived and only brought to light again during the investigation for his cause for canonization. It was published in Italian in 2009 and received some attention, but again, it fell out of the public eye.

Given the love the Polish people have for St. John Paul II, it may seem surprising that The Rule never "took off" in Poland. Yet, as one man remembered, the Polish people preferred to continue on with their informal community with *Wujek* on a more personal level rather than formalize it into an official movement. This man recalled:

> At that time *Wujek* proposed the model of a French family movement (*The Rule*). That idea, however, didn't catch. Why didn't we care about a training movement? Maybe we

thought that the same contact with
*Wujek* would 'fix' everything?[49]

They did not feel they needed anything formal
because they had this holy man right there in their
lives. As Fr. Kwiatkowski, one of the authors of the
Italian publication (and the one who brought to light
these rediscovered texts), explains, "the conciseness
and brevity of the text, as well as the somewhat
complex history of the same initiative, have made it
practically unknown."[50] And so it has stayed...until
now.

The Rule has six simple points that contain nine
elements of the groups' commitment: Community,
'The Real & the Ideal', *Humanae Vitae*, Marriage Unity,
Christian Morality, Conjugal Spirituality, Studying
Marriage, Apostolate, and Prayer. Through The Rule,
couples can find extraordinary strength in their
spousal love and be lifted beyond the struggle and into
joy, even as they carry their own little crosses.

## First Point: COMMUNITY. THE REAL AND THE IDEAL. *HUMANAE VITAE*

The writing of The Rule itself is an affirmation of
the need for community. Couples aren't meant to pray
through on their own; The Rule is to form Married
Couple *Groups*. We need each other in order to stand

---

[49] Przemyslaw Kwiatkowski, *Lo Sposo Passa Per Questa Strada: La spiritualità coniugale nel pensiero di Karol Wojtyła. Le origini*, (Cantagalli: Siena, 2011), 116.
[50] Grygiel, 16.

strong against the flood of secular culture. When we support each other, we are not alone, and the journey becomes a little easier. Together in Christ, we find our strength.

The first point explains that The Rule came from real experiences of married couples in Fr. Wojtyła's pastoral ministry. This emphasizes that we cannot take theology (the *Ideal*) apart from our experience (the *Real*). We must keep both pieces in mind at all times. We will see later, in one of the accompanying texts, that he says we should always keep in mind this *"integral vision of the person."* We must see each person in two moments: *who he is* and *who he ought to be*. Sometimes we think we can't participate in something because we are not good enough; we struggle too much. But the struggle is a sign of holiness, not weakness. We must stop and acknowledge the actual challenges that others are experiencing (the *Real*). We all have broken bits in our lives, but "(w)e are not the sum of our weaknesses and failures; we are the sum of the Father's love for us and our real capacity to become the image of his Son."[51] While we sympathize, listen, and care for spouses in their realness, we do not leave them there. We lovingly call each other to holiness (the *Ideal*). When we seek union with Christ, that pursuit of holiness itself lightens the crosses we carry.

---

[51] JOHN PAUL II Apostolic visit to Toronto, to Cuidad de Guatemala and to Cuidad de Mexico - 17th World Youth Day - Solemn Mass - HOMILY OF THE HOLY FATHER JOHN PAUL II - Toronto, Downsview Park, Sunday July 28, 2002.

This first point also tells us that the teaching of *Humanae Vitae* is core and, in fact, the reason The Rule was written. The Rule was inspired by *Humanae Vitae* and helps couples bring this *Ideal* into the *Real* of everyday, married life. St. John Paul II affirms that "*Humanae Vitae* ... proposes new authentically Christian — therefore evangelical — practices for the spouses and their pastors."[52] He even recommends that these groups be given the name '*Humanae Vitae.*'

## Second Point: MARRIAGE UNITY.

The second point explains that the *Unity of husband and wife* is vital to their life of joy. He goes so far as to say that one spouse cannot participate in a group without the other. Both spouses must be committed to the group and to growing in holiness. (We will see that this dual commitment is crucial for building conjugal spirituality, which is mentioned in point four.)

## Third Point: CHRISTIAN MORALITY.

The third point explains that the couples are being called to live according to the *Commandments and the norms of Christian morality*. This is not an extraordinary calling, but as we have seen mentioned before, even living a normal Christian marriage in a progressively anti-Christian culture takes a higher commitment of

---

[52] *The Rule*, point 1.

faith. (This is why community is so important.) He also encourages us to live the *spirit* of the evangelical counsels (poverty, chastity, and obedience). St. John Paul II is not a micromanager. He does not specify exactly what this will look like in a particular marriage but that each couple in the group should reflect on how the spirit of these counsels can be put into practice in their own marriages and in their family life.

# Fourth Point: CONJUGAL SPIRITUALITY. STUDYING MARRIAGE.

The fourth point of The Rule explains the primary purpose for these groups: that each couple cultivate the spiritual attitude mentioned above so that the teaching on marriage by Jesus Christ and further explained by the Church "could be accomplished in their married life with full understanding and full love."[53] It is here that St. John Paul II points to the need to *constantly learn about the truth of marriage*.

He also touches upon conjugal spirituality when he says that for this truth of marriage to be actualized or accomplished in a particular marriage, the couple must form an "appropriate spirituality — or an internal life."[54] It might be a bit startling that he says a married couple should have one interior life, but remember this is the *Ideal*. This "appropriate spirituality" is what allows husband and wife to shape their marriage and

---

[53] *Ibid.*, point 4.
[54] *Ibid.*

family life in a truly Christian way. Each couple is encouraged to keep striving for holiness, and as they do so, because of their sacramental marriage, they will form *one interior life*. It is a profound spiritual unity.

What is so interesting is that this isn't an over-spiritualization of married life. This conjugal spirituality is as real at the kneeler in church as it is folding laundry, or caring for your children, or paying your bills. What we learn about the *Ideal* of marriage must be brought into the *Real* of life, allowing the love of Christ to penetrate all aspects of our marriage (no matter how mundane they seem). The explanation of conjugal spirituality often found in the other texts and how it can bring about this profound spiritual unity is nothing short of breathtaking.

You can read more about conjugal spirituality in part 2.

## Fifth Point: APOSTOLATE. PRAYER.

The fifth point of The Rule sends the group of married couples outward in love. The Married Couple Group must have an apostolate, yet this is not predetermined but should be decided upon by the group. This allows each group to develop their own charism—what is most important to them as a whole. Some groups may feel called to serve the youth ministry in their parish, while others may choose to spend their apostolate assisting a pro-life ministry or serving the poor. It is important that the group serves in this way together, thus strengthening the community between them. In the accompanying texts, St. John Paul II explains how these communities will be like a sort of "seminary for marriage," a novitiate for the youth to see what Christian marriage is. This emphasis may also point to each group's apostolate incorporating the support of marriage in some way.

In addition to the apostolate, the group is called to *prayer*. The Rule states that the group should pray specifically for:
- The other couples in their group
- Married couples in general
-For the truth of marriage and family to be understood in the Church and in the world.

The method of prayer a group uses is left up to the group.

## Sixth Point: COMMITMENT.

The sixth point of The Rule emphasizes the *commitment* each couple ought to have toward their group. For a community to truly be a family of families, the couples need to be able to count on one another for support. St. John Paul II states that each group must decide how they will accomplish all of these six goals through a written commitment or promise. This is not another program to add to our life or a Bible study (both of which are good in their own right). This is a way of life; it is a community of married couples spiritually supporting each other so that together they may all rise to the higher level of "moral perfection"[55] needed to live an authentically Christian marriage in a progressively anti-Christian culture.

You can read more about all these topics in *Part Two: Going Deeper*.

---

[55] *Reflections on Marriage, 3. Economy and Personalism*

# 5

# THE RULE FOR MARRIED COUPLES GROUP *HUMANAE VITAE* (THE PREMISES)[56] – BY CARDINAL KAROL WOJTYŁA

1. The below Rule is born based on pastoral experiences working with married couples as well as experiences of those married couples themselves. It is created in the moment of the publishing of the encyclical *Humanae Vitae*, which proposes new, authentically Christian—therefore, evangelical—practices for the spouses and their pastors. The group of the married couples that adapts this Rule could call themselves "Humanae Vitae."

---

[56] K. WOJTYŁA, "Reguła dla grupy małżeństw *Humanae vitae* (założenia)", in AWDR M 23. (AWDR – an official abbreviation of the Archives of the Office of the Metropolitan Curia of Krakow for family and pastoral care – *Archiwum Wydziału Duszpasterstwa Rodzin Kurii Metropolitalnej w Krakowie*). Translated by A. Pata, 2020.

2. The Rule applies only to the married couples and not to the single spouses. It must be accepted and realized by both partners in the conjugal relationship, not by husband or wife alone without the participation and engagement of their spouse.

3. The Rule expects from the spouses to live according to the principles of Christian morality based on the order of the commandments; it does not commit them to live by the strict rules of evangelical counsels. Implementing the evangelical counsels of poverty, chastity, and obedience in their strict meaning is required only from those with a religious vocation. Nevertheless, the experience of conjugal life indicates that living by the moral principles declared by the Church is not possible without certain asceticism; therefore, the married couples in the group "Humanae Vitae" must reflect on how to apply the spirit of the evangelical counsels in their lives.

4. The specific goal of the "Humanae Vitae" group is the continuous commitment to reach such spiritual attitude where the integral teachings of Jesus Christ on marriage and family, proclaimed by the Church, could be accomplished in their married life with full understanding and full love. It is a matter of forming the appropriate spirituality — or an internal life — which allows to configure the conjugal and family life in a Christian way. Such spirituality does not exist in a definitive form like the ones of the different convents; instead it must be constantly reworked. The reworking on this spirituality also is the important task for the group of the married couples. The means to

accomplish this is by putting the above-described spiritual attitude in practice by the spouses.

5. The second goal of the group is the apostolate. We do not specify here what form it needs to take. However, the married couples of the group must take on the role of certain apostolate, and, most of all, an obligation to pray for the other married couples and for the idea of marriage and family in the contemporary church and in the world. Just like the forms of apostolate, the forms of these prayers are to be developed progressively.

6. It is up to the married couples themselves to decide whether, and when, to take the special vow to commit to the outlined tasks.

# 6

## THE RULE IN ACTION

When we ourselves first came upon The Rule in the Italian translation, we were surprised such a thing existed and even more surprised that it was virtually unknown! Having helped many engaged and married couples, we have witnessed firsthand the struggle they face while attempting to live out their faith. In fact, we have experienced this struggle ourselves. We have been searching for something to help assist couples, to help them get beyond the white-knuckling of their faith and truly find lasting joy.

As we noted earlier, it is one thing to understand why a teaching is true, but it is different to know how to live out that teaching joyfully in our lives. We may attend a talk on marriage, or maybe we'll learn *Theology of the Body,* or attend a marriage retreat, and our hearts are lifted. We hear the truth and we are filled with peace. Then, we'll return home and within minutes, life will smack us back to reality—we will fold laundry, clean Play-Doh from the grooves of the wooden table, and wipe mud from our boots—and it feels so distant from the beautiful *Ideal* we have just heard. For years, we have tried to find a way to help spouses more easily bring the Ideal into the Real of their messy, daily lives. When we saw The Rule, our hearts swelled! We thought, "Finally! This is it! This is the key!"

The Rule by St. John Paul II is the gift he left for our generation — *just waiting to be unwrapped!*

The Rule is not anything extreme, but it helps focus couples on the elements that matter most in their path to holiness. Everything about The Rule is pointed towards deepening the spouses' relationship with God, drawing us in to the heart of the Father, and saturating our love in divine love. Oftentimes, spouses sell themselves short of their God-given potential, because they don't even know it is possible. Can you imagine the wellspring of renewal the Church would experience, if countless couples were able to cross that threshold into lasting joy, and pour that joy and witness to divine love back into their children and the people around them?!

You may be thinking right now of all you have been through on your spiritual journey thus far — the joys, sorrows, and wounds — and whether holiness is really possible. Remember: God sees you. He sees all your great efforts, your failings, your frustrations, and your desire to love Him no matter what. *He sees you.* He loves you more intensely than you could ever fathom! He is with you right now. You are not alone.

It can sometimes feel like we are though, right? With every stride in faith, another wave can push in against us. The nightly news can be stressful, work can feel overbearing, and friends who you thought believed Christ's teaching begin fighting against it. Yet, St. John Paul II tells us, "I plead with you! Never, ever give up on hope, never doubt, never tire, and never become discouraged. Be not afraid."[57]

So, how do we do this? How do we live with heroic virtue and never give up hope in our times? St. John Paul II states that it is through the support of community. As we will see in one of the accompanying texts in part 2, he states that when there is no community that upholds the culture of the person and encourages conjugal spirituality, then it must be created.[58]

Our hearts were moved to respond to this plea. We are delighted to share with you that in honor of this beloved saint, and in acknowledgement of the time in his life when he offered this pastoral guide of The Rule, we have founded the Wojtyła Community & Institute, Inc (WCI).

# Wojtyła Community & Institute

The WCI was founded on the fifty-second anniversary of *Humanae Vitae* in 2020. It is an intentional, committed, Catholic community

---

[57] St. John Paul II, World Youth Day, 1993.
[58] Cf. *Reflections on Marriage, 2. Education on Marriage, culture of the person.*

implementing The Rule of St. John Paul II. Our mission statement (and rallying cry) is: "Trusting *The Rule* of St. John Paul II, we are a family of families, striving for holiness, strengthening marriages and living the truth of *Humanae Vitae* with Joy!" Our goal is JOY-fully actualizing the teachings of the Church within the life of the married couple through conjugal spirituality and community.

WCI Married Couple Groups, following The Rule, help spouses transition from acceptance of the teachings of the Church into a profound orientation of their lives to Christ — and a closeness to the heart of the Father within their marriage that they never before thought possible. Divine love enters in — and changes everything. With the grace of God, following The Rule helps couples be more receptive to God's love, and Love enters in to every aspect of their married life. They are able to live their Christian lives with great joy. The Rule helps good couples become great through God's grace.

*What a gift St. John Paul II has left for us!*

One of the aspects of The Rule that is so important to the WCI is *the Real and the Ideal.* We strive to always see each human person in those two moments: "who man is" and "who man ought to be." We understand the real struggles of life and acknowledge the emotional, physical, and spiritual toll these challenges take on a couple. Couples are able to let their guard down and share honestly. If we don't allow the realness to be shared — even if it may be a little humbling — then we cannot support each other in our journey. Only in seeing ourselves in all our present rawness can God show us where we need to grow.

We must humbly recognize that we all have muck; we are all broken. St. John Paul II was known for his loving gaze towards others. His gaze made them feel they were the only one in the world and that whatever they were experiencing, they were loved. We pray for that same ability to love attentively — first our spouse, then others. St. John Paul II reminds us that we must not leave each other there. We must recognize *the real* and also lovingly encourage each other toward Christian perfection and holiness: the ideal. We must not be afraid of this messy middle of life when accompanying couples on the road to holiness.

We discuss the WCI more at the end of the book. If you would like to learn more, please visit us at **wojtylaci.com**.

# Be Not Afraid!

Living a faithful Christian marriage today does, indeed, take courage. However, the result of lasting, authentic joy in one's life is a goal worthy of the sacrifice. When a couple can, in their unity, be drawn into the 'orbit of grace' with the Blessed Trinity; wrapped in divine love—Love that renews their spousal love; perfects their individuality; enters into every fiber of their union; and remakes them—born again into His divine life; they walk on the earth, but they live in Heaven and find great and lasting joy. When divine love has kissed a marriage, no cross will be too heavy to bear. The pleasures of the modern world then lose their grip upon the spouses' souls, for they pale in comparison to the rapture of union with God.

John Paul II said, "the future of marriage ... depends on each and every one of us."[59] It is up to all of us to build up marriages so they might pour life back into our world. Following The Rule is a way of life that does not detract from life but helps fortify and strengthen it. The future of marriage is indeed in the hands of not a few but all the faithful.

We must commit to the challenging balance of meeting others in the realness of life and encouraging them to strive toward Christian perfection and toward He who is truth, Jesus Christ. And in Christ our Lord, we will find abundant joy!

The time is now.

A new dawn of Catholicism awaits; let us march forward and **be not afraid.**

---

[59] *Reflection on Marriage, 2. Education on Marriage – the culture of a person.*

FR. KAROL WOJTYŁA (ST. JOHN PAUL II) ON A HIKING
TRIP WITH FRIENDS.[60]

[60] This photo is used with permission from the Director of the
Karol Wojtyła Chair; its duplication is forbidden without explicit
permission from the Director of the Karol Wojtyła Chair.

## ST. JOHN PAUL II'S HANDWRITTEN DRAFT OF THE RULE.

4. Celem właściwym grupy małżeństw „Stowarzyszał stał" jest stały wysiłek zmierzający do takiej postawy duchowej, aby nauka Chrystusa Pana o małżeństwie i rodzinie głoszona przez Kościół mogła być w ich małżeństwie z całym zrozumieniem i [...] umiłowaniem wypełniana.

Chodzi więc o kształtowanie właściwej duchowości — typ życia wewnętrznego — które pozwoli na to, by życie małżeńskie i rodzinne było układane [...] po chrześcijańsku. Duchowość taka nie istnieje w formie gotowej tak jak duchowość [...] różnych zakonów, ale musi zostać wypracowana. Wypracowanie takiej duchowości jest również ważnym zadaniem grupy małżeństw zdolnym do [...] jej praktykowania przez [...] małżeństwa grupy owej postawy duchowej, o którą nowa powyżej.

5. Drugim właściwym celem grupy jest apostolstwo, jakie one [...] formy. I tutaj nie rozstrzygamy. W każdym razie małżeństwa grupy biorą na siebie obowiązek pewnego apostolstwa, a przede wszystkim obowiązek stałej modlitwy za inne małżeństwa oraz za cały wielki problem, jakim [...] [...] Kościół, i [...] jest małżeństwo. Zarówno konkretna forma apostolstwa, jak i formy modlitwy, o której mowa jest [...] sprawą do obopólnego [...] [...].

6. Do rozstrzygnięcia samych samych zainteresowanych małżeństw pozostaje w, czy i w jakim czasie [...] w do [...] tutaj zadań [...] [...] specjalnym przyrzeczeniem.

# PART TWO

# GOING DEEPER

# 7

# INTRODUCTION TO THE TWO ACCOMPANYING TEXTS

You made it to part 2! We are so glad you did. An adventure awaits. You now have a basic idea of how The Rule helps configure spouses' hearts be open to the grace of the sacrament of marriage. St. John Paul II's goal, in his emphasis on continuing education on marriage, is that this understanding will not stop in your mind but pierce your heart. God, the ineffable Blessed Trinity, our Father, our Bridegroom Messiah Jesus Christ, the powerful and gentle Spirit—God Himself—desires to unite Himself with you.

The Rule speaks of a conjugal spirituality that unites spouses so profoundly to the Blessed Trinity that they share one interior life. This fundamental shift in their souls, which draws them into the heart of the Father, is an extraordinary grace given to ordinary persons. The benefits of St. John Paul II's Married Couple Groups are felt in the support of this little community that uplifts couples past the struggle against the culture and past the temptations in their own hearts and places them on a clearer path. This is not a magic trick. It's not something automatic like a snack machine—place in your prayers and group meetings and out pops amazing growth instantly. It takes time to understand The Rule. It takes time to allow what you learn to affect your heart, your marriage, your life. Each group must entrust themselves to our Blessed Mother, commit to following The Rule, and strive to open their hearts more to the grace of God.

There is so much to say about the benefits of living The Rule that can barely be put into words; movements of the heart can be difficult to explain. When we open our hearts more to God's grace through what we've learned and what we've shared, it affects us, and we feel immensely loved. Yet even here, we do not fully understand. This second half of the book is meant to help you peel back the layers even more, unearth what all this means, and understand how it could affect your marriage. When an ordinary marriage clears the path for extraordinary grace, Love breaks in, crushing away what is not of God, and opening a path to eternal joy. Throughout this book, we have used the word *joy* often, and perhaps it loses its full significance. What kind of joy do we mean? Our hearts are opened to a joy that is unfettered, unblemished, and untarnished by sadness. A joy that does not blot out suffering but puts it on display like the wounds in the hands of the Risen Christ—triumphant joy! It is a joy that feels as if you touched heaven and never want to leave. A joy that makes you forget yourself and only wish ever more to live for God. When Love breaks in, everything changes.

As we dig into these two additional texts of St. John Paul II, we are moving in deeper so we can better understand this Rule and this path into the heart of the Father. We'll learn from the professor, pastor, and pope. We'll allow this knowledge to teach us how to let Love break in.

The texts that we have translated for you from the original Polish are also being published here in English for the first time. The Rule for Married Couple Groups is succinct, so we can use these two contemporary texts of his, which also were written between 1957 and 1969, to help us understand the ideas and themes that The Rule presumes. If you recall, we highlighted nine themes within The Rule: Community, 'The Real and the Ideal', *Humanae Vitae*, Marriage Unity, Christian Morality, Conjugal Spirituality, Studying Marriage, Apostolate, and Prayer.

We have designed this second part to introduce these texts then allow you to dive into each of the themes as you are ready. Be courageous! St. John Paul II has quite an intellect, and the texts can be heavy. Yet his wisdom, as always, is breathtaking and priceless.

You will also meet some of the couples who are already living The Rule in Married Couple Groups. We hope their experiences will further help illuminate how to follow The Rule and the graces that come from it in time. Through their stories, we help theology meet experience, as St. John Paul II said was so important.

We will start with a quick summary, then St. John Paul II's text, and then we will spend some time "unpacking" the texts. Many have found that reading through the explanations allow you to understand the translations with a better grasp. As a side note, when we worked with the translator, we chose a direct translation approach. This means that the English translation is as close to the Polish as possible. This helps preserve St. John Paul II's words as they are passed to us, but it occasionally makes the English a little, well, inelegant. We were willing to accept this, though, in order to stay as true to St. John Paul II's original writing as possible.

# 8

# "REFLECTIONS ON MARRIAGE"[61]

## Synopsis

The first accompanying text was written by Father Wojtyła in 1957, eleven years prior to the promulgation of *Humanae Vitae* and one year before his ordination to the episcopate. This was written when he was engaged with the *Środowisko* community.[62] In this letter, he takes the Feast of the Nativity of Our Lord (Christmas) to reflect on the Incarnation and how this mystery deepens our understanding of the sacrament of marriage. Our Christian faith is founded upon the mystery of the Incarnation, St. John Paul II explains, and God being "made flesh" signifies that every part of what is human, "all the things of the flesh — all the things that establish human corporality and are visibly complete in the human body, they entered the orbit of this new fact," of God made man.[63]

---

[61] K. WOJTYŁA, "Myśli o małżeństwie", in *Znak* 7 (1957) 595–604. Translated by A. Pata, 2020.

[62] Find the story of this community in part I, chapter 3.

[63] *Reflections on Marriage, 1. At the Foundations of Personalism.*

# Reflections on Marriage –
## by Fr. Karol Wojtyła[64]

The Feast of the Nativity of Our Lord is a holiday that, for us particularly, is of a family nature. It is not coincidental but well-founded, and with roots that go deeper than most people expect. We talk here about the believers, or at the least those who live in the circle of influence of Christian thought. In Poland, as we know, these people are numerous. We realize this each year during the Feast of the Nativity. It would not make sense to assume that, as the evening of Christmas Eve approaches, the religious challenges disappear and the worldview of all people in Poland becomes Christian. Certainly, it is not so. However, we cannot deny that Christmas is this time that reveals its particular dimension in which people are met with the Christian truth despite their challenged beliefs or even denial in that field. In the below reflections we will try to capture and deepen our understanding of it. This understanding must be theological by nature. Its object cannot be understood in a different way. Even an atheist needs to acknowledge the competence of a theologian, even if they do not agree on the *meritum* of their reflections.

It is necessary to capture this special dimension of common thinking of so many people in order to create a base on which to analyze, at least in part, the fundamental question of human life. This article will

---

[64] K. WOJTYŁA, "Myśli o małżeństwie", in *Znak* 7 (1957) 595-604. Translated by A. Pata, 2020.

speak about the sacrament of marriage: It will attempt a commensurate link to the truth of Christmas (which we will explain below). Marriage, as a fruitful, life-giving communion of two people, as the base of the family, is always in a certain way a sacrament – that is, something marked by God, the Creator and Life-Giver. An atheist will not admit this truth in all its entirety but by considering marriage to be a life-giving communion of people – and that is undeniable – we already think alike and, in a certain but fundamental way, we find the common ground to discuss these matters.

The below reflections are a theological elaboration on some fundamental human questions. The theological elaboration does not take away its human character, though. Just the opposite, it will highlight it. We must just free ourselves of any prejudice. This will allow us to see the same matters in the dimension that is revealed each year during Christmas.

## 1. *At the Foundations of Personalism*

Christianity grows on the basis of the mystery of the Incarnation. God the Son, assuming a human nature, "was made flesh" the same way each human is flesh. Therefore, all the things of the flesh – all the things that establish human corporality and are visibly complete in the human body – they entered the orbit of this new fact. Let us, first of all, note that in this fact their human content has been confirmed in a new way. In the conscience of a believer, the meaning of this confirmation is uplifting, stunning, but also overwhelming. To explore the content of this confirmation – this affirmation – let's distinguish between the three orders that emanate from the mystery of the Incarnation: the order of person, the order of grace, and the order of sacrament.

a. *The Order of Person*. It is worth recalling that the mystery of the Incarnation caused numerous controversies and inquiries into the relationship between person and nature in the first centuries of Christianity. It regarded a certain comprehension — one that is accessible to human reason — of the mysteries of God: in three divine persons and God Incarnate. These inquiries brought the kind of study of God's nature that never again has been seen in the history of the Church. It resulted in the development of a fundamental concept of person, which, in relation to nature, always represents a being spiritually individualized and free. This spiritual dimension of reason and freedom belongs exclusively to the person. Nature can be rational (i.e., endowed with reason and free will), only when it exists in the person as a specific subject of being and acting.

At the time, all these reflections and affirmations were referring to the divine reality. Nevertheless, they formed a basis to a deeper understanding of man and introduced *personalism* into the human sciences. The mere fact that human personalism was based on the groundwork of knowledge about God, on the basis of the mystery of the Incarnation, is of great significance. It brings a Christian coloring to personalism. There is a fundamental link between God and man due to the fact that man is a person and God is also, in a special way, a person — the divine nature lives in the incomprehensible tri-personality. This link, based on this similarity, does not ignore the total disparity between God's and man's nature; it creates, however, the grounds for thinking about the existence of an element God's nature within human nature. Following the fall of Adam, it is exactly in the mystery of the Incarnation — in the birth of Christ — that mankind can look for the foundations of this identity.

b. *The Order of Grace* explains this link. Grace brings man closer to God. This objective proximity to God equals holiness; therefore, grace sanctifies. It sanctifies by infusing the nature of the soul and its faculties with the elements of God's life. These are real characteristics that can be called sanctifying grace, faith, hope, love — gifts of the Holy Spirit and which are the leaven of a person's new life. In its spiritual life, a person benefits from these gifts that were implanted in its nature in the form of grace. By taking advantage of grace, a person leads a new spiritual life — life that is supernatural; supernatural to what degree depends on this person's actualization of the resources of grace in his or her life. Thanks to this, the relationship of human person to the tri-personal God becomes proper. In this way, the man-person relationship to the triune God becomes appropriate (i.e., one that corresponds to the Creator's plans and purposes for humanity).

These reflections allow a better understanding of the problem of the sacrament of marriage. The energy of the super-nature — of grace — are hidden in the nature, or in the natures, of persons that connect through marriage. These forces may be active on a lower or higher degree. This degree of their actualization decides the holiness of man, his objective proximity to God, the degree of unity with Him. The degree of actualization of the supernatural forces in people united in marriage determines the sanctity of their union and their proximity to God. Man is in the first instance, as it were, close to God, similar to Him by the fact that he has a personality. In the second instance, by saturating the life of a person with supernatural elements. Matrimony, at first instance, is also close to God by being a union of persons based on love. There is also a certain analogy with the union of Persons that we find in Holy Trinity. At a higher instance, there is a matrimony that is close to God as a union of love between persons, man and woman, based on the mystery of the Incarnation — the mystery of grace that penetrates into nature. This is exactly the Christian sacrament of marriage. It shows marriage to be a human reality that is deeply rooted in God through the mystery of the Incarnation. And it is exactly the fact that uplifts and illuminates but can also overwhelm and frighten, especially when confronted with a well-known weakness of people who live in extraordinary closeness with God.

c. *The Order of Sacrament.* It is precisely this human weakness that, in a special way, explains the order of sacrament. Through the mystery of the Incarnation, God entered into the totality of the human nature; therefore also the "flesh", which in a certain sense is its synonym. This way the "flesh" — the body of Man-Christ — became a visible sign and a prototype of all such signs. For centuries now, the Church has named them sacraments. A sacrament is a visible and effective sign of grace: a man that is "flesh", through a sacrament, becomes part of what is divine, what is supernatural in its matter. It is as if every sacrament, in its essence, reproduced the Incarnation at a reduced dimension, at the scale of the person; or, when we talk about a marriage, at the scale of two persons. Incarnation repeats and, at the same time, lengthens and extends; because Incarnation is supposed to extend to all men, letting them all participate in the adoption as sons of God, in the image of God, the Son Incarnate.

The sacrament, as an effective sign of grace, creates in nature supernatural forces, forces that allow for a full life of a human being — that is to say, life according to the plans and intentions of the Creator towards the mankind. These forces make such a life possible for the human person but not what achieves it. It is then necessary to extract from these forces everything that is hidden in it and apply it to the personal life. This is already the task of man, or people who, through the sacrament, enter the orbit of grace.

This fact is of particular importance when it comes to the sacrament of matrimony because there are simultaneously two persons that enter the orbit of grace. Moreover, their entry into the orbit of grace, the very one created by the sacrament of marriage, they always owe this to one another. After all, they are the ministers of this sacrament: If one of them didn't bring in the expression of their autonomous and mature decision, there would be no sacrament, and, with it, there would be no grace — the very grace which the sacrament of marriage creates in people. These two persons are for each other direct instruments of the action of God. They are like conductors to the current of life that is in God and of which they become partakers through the sacrament.

Let us bring together all that has been said above about the order of grace and the order of person, and we will have a full vision of Christian marriage. This vision presupposed in all its depths the mystery of the Incarnation, its content, and its specific dynamics. Only a man that is capable of attaining this vision to some extent, will also be able to grasp the objective sanctity of a Christian marriage and to recognize with all all his conviction the reasons for its indissolubility.

## 2. *Education for Marriage – the Culture of the Person*

Every man must recognize that the main problem of marriage is the problem of the person. In essence, marriage is a union of two persons and not just their combination or connection based on sex-appeal of two different natures—male and female. Marriage is, undoubtedly, this connection of natures, but this alone does not determine its human specificity. The proper basis of their love, to which a marriage owes its origin and existence, is not in their natures alone—in their psychophysical diverse sexuality. Human love is always an act of the person, and it is directed toward another person. The vast series of psychophysical manifestations accompany, and even determine this love, but they cannot overshadow its principal personal character. Love does not allow itself to be broken down into all these manifestations or into their sum; therefore it does not allow itself to be completely limited to them. It constitutes its wholeness just like man is his wholeness. And man in his totality is a person, and love, as an act of a man — seen integrally and profoundly — is always an act of a person.

This character of the person and this character of human love is grasped and explained at its very core only by philosophy. Specific sciences require certain disintegration, certain methodical breakdown of the totality of the human being into a series of matters and aspects, to analyze them separately, to establish the regularity of each one of them. Consequently, physiology can examine one of the factors of human sexual love, but alone it cannot determine its essence in all its fullness, it can only illuminate it from a certain point of view. Such illumination is precious for the understanding of love, but it is not enough. Psychology will illuminate the same issue from a different angle, but it also will not be able to capture its full content, although it seems to bring it closer than physiological sexology. Yet another perspective can be presented by sociology as it will illuminate the social background of the issue, but it also will need to assume the physiological concept of the person and of love.

The propaedeutic[65] of marriage means educating people, women and men, to that specific maturity which marriage requires. This type of propaedeutic must be based on knowledge; therefore it must combine everything that physiology, psychology, sociology, or any other science say about sexual life, love, and family. However, all these elements must be

---

[65] Editor's note: *Propaedutic* is an older term that means a preparatory study or instruction.

then integrated by submitting them to the person, to man in his totality.

For this reason, *ethics* must play a major role in the propaedeutics of marriage. There are two ways ethics approaches problems: one is from the aspect of norms themselves, their formal content and the logical connections between them; the other way is from the aspect of the subject to whom these norms refer (i.e., from the aspect of man and his actions). In both cases, as ethics approaches a specific problem, all the aspects of human science must be submitted to the person. Ethics presupposes an integral person, it implies his total, and at the same time, specific potentiality. That is why it must be the essential dimension of the propaedeutic of marriage, as well as the propaedeutic of any other aspect of human life. It is important that ethics sees a man-person (*nota bene* within the full framework of social life) constantly in two moments: who he is and who he ought to be. It is driven by an integral vision of man, perfect man – a vision that other specific sciences lack.

It is on the basis of this dual vision of a man in ethics that the doctrine of virtues is born; it is a study of qualities relative only to the person, qualities that make the person good as a person, that make a person's life good in different respects. Such doctrine could not be born of any other human science but the one which sees man in his entirety: actual and potential.

Thanks to the doctrine of virtues, aretalogy, ethics becomes the fundamental part—the only adequate basis—for education. The propaedeutic of marriage, that is, the education of persons to the maturity needed in marriage, is essentially a matter of virtue. But it has been known since at least the time of Aristotle that the road leading from the study on virtues to the actual living out of the human virtues is quite long. That road runs through the areas of will, through the spheres of human emotions and drives, therefore the areas studied also by physiologists and psychologists. All their discoveries will be integrated through ethics and its peculiar vision of a man in two moments: who he is and who he should be. The understanding of the person is a factor without which not even the most modern results of experimental sciences, physiology, psychology, or sociology will ever contribute to the propaedeutic of marriage. In fact, they could even destroy this work, narrow it down. Marriage demands, above all, the culture of the person.

What is "culture of the person?" Without giving a straight answer, let us just say that one cannot have and practice it without a strong and well-grounded vision of the person, his being, his capabilities (high and low), his destiny. This vision depends, among other things, on whether the sexual love itself will be at the level of the dignity of the person. Obviously, it is not a question of theorizing about the person but of the fact that the vision of the person continues to shape everything that lies in the propaedeutic of marriage as well as of marriage itself.

Propaedeutic of marriage is certainly a duty of the society: of the whole society in a larger and indirect meaning but in a closer and direct sense — of that part of the society that can call itself the community. In the times when the culture of the person diminishes in the society — something that may progress, and sometimes at frightening dimensions, in parallel with growth of material wealth, or rather excess — there are no means for the propaedeutic of marriage other than creating communities in which the culture of a person can grow. Such communities will fulfill their role despite any setbacks and failures. At the same time, it is important to make the entire society aware, everyone possible, that the future of marriage, the future of all and each individual marriage, depends on each and every one of us, on the level of culture of the person in all of us.

Propaedeutic of the *sacrament* of marriage is a slightly separate problem. In Christian societies it is associated simply with propaedeutic of marriage itself, which does not mean, however, that we cannot or should not highlight certain differences. Although there is no doubt that a Christian marriage based on the sacrament must, first of all, be healthy in the natural sense, its sacramentality nevertheless brings in certain new content that could not be recognized without the study of the mystery of the Incarnation. Based on this mystery of the Gospel, the culture of the person takes on new meanings. The propaedeutic of the sacrament of marriage consists of absorbing these meanings, and their assimilation within the thoughts, the heart and the will of each interested person. Since it is the entire Christian society that is implicitly interested, it too in its totality must fundamentally assimilate the sense of the fact that God the Son "was made flesh."

When the Christian society acknowledges that, despite appearances, these meanings are not assimilated, that the contents and values in the sacrament of marriage based on the sacrament of the Incarnation have died in life, practice and motivation behind peoples' actions, it then needs to take on the burden of assimilating these meanings, contents and values — from the beginning. It would become a sort of re-education in the field of the sacrament of marriage. The matter of the propaedeutic of the sacrament of marriage becomes, in that instance, a particularly important duty for the society, primarily for all those who realize the gravity of this matter. And most likely the best method is again a method of building communities in which the propaedeutic of the sacrament of marriage can be developed as a social function and as a resultant of activity of different members of the specific community.

We all see that this is exactly the direction of different initiatives among Catholic societies in the West. In Poland there is still a weak awareness of the need for such re-education, and that a need certainly exists, especially in the circles of intellectuals, whose considerations of the marriage are eclectic, rather than authentically Christian. The adjective "Christian" means in this case, "according to the needs of the person," "personalistic," therefore "human."

Methodology of the initiatives toward re-education may be diverse, but they all must ultimately refer to this one method: to the culture of the person. In the fully Christian approach, this culture is born on such vision of the person, his being, his capabilities and his destiny that can be found in the content and objective dynamic of the mystery of the Incarnation.

3. *Economy and Personalism*

In our times, the entire question of the propaedeutic of marriage, and most of all, of the propaedeutic of the sacrament of marriage, carries yet another aspect of great importance. That is a socio-economic aspect. It is not to say that it was not important in other times in history, but today it is clearly more notable. Without entering too much in the socio-economic details of the structure of a modern marriage and family, I wish to bring attention to one thing which is, in my opinion, central.

It is clear that humankind has gone through massive economic changes. These changes, as of today, have brought enormous challenges to conjugal and family life. It is enough to recall such typical examples as: the necessity for both spouses to work professionally (with all its consequences on family life and children upbringing), the lack of material means necessary to start and support a family, and the most acute, especially in large cities, the lack of housing. Observing these facts and their consequences on morality, particularly the moral life of married couples and families, we must think of one practical truth, one rule that the Church tested in its activities a long time ago. According to this rule, collectivization requires a particular moral maturity from those who decide to take part in it. Without high moral standards it becomes very dangerous. In turn, according to the implications of materialism, economic relations are to result in a new changed morality which will be the effect of the new system. All the while, Christianity is still convinced that living in a community requires, above all, high moral standards in which the spiritual ideal enables renunciation from a certain type of material goods — or from a certain relationship with these goods. Such spiritual ideal is not born mechanically, thanks to the changed economic conditions, but needs to be created — as always in the case of moral values — thanks to the efforts of the human person within the society.

So far, the economic conditions have only hindered this work on the culture of the person that constitutes the core of married and family life. But such statement will not be of much good. It is truly more important to realize that the changed socio-economic conditions simply require an even higher culture of the person so that the marriage and family could live on moral levels necessary for their human and Christian character. This is how we must present this issue. Any other representation of this matter will not serve any purpose, will not solve anything, and will only serve as explanation of failures and defeats in this field. Christian society remains surprised by these transformations and economic relations, which an ordinary human morality in many cases cannot cope with. The consequence of this surprise is a number of failures or even disasters in the moral life of marriages and families. We cannot accept this. The events that took place from the economic perspective are forcing us to intensify our efforts in the moral dimension related to the culture of the person in the life of a marriage and family. Sometimes, we speak of the need for heroism in this area. Such words are not an exaggeration.

Certainly, in ordinary conditions men cannot be obliged to heroism, but there are certain extraordinary conditions that may demand it of him. Even a very general look at this situation forces us to admit that a full culture of the person in the life of a marriage and family, in current socio-economic conditions, can be accomplished at the cost of efforts not entirely ordinary, but extraordinary. Tough as it may be, we must look the truth in the eyes and engage this severely true fact into the system of the propaedeutic of the sacrament of marriage.

Whereas in these days we still cannot confuse and tangle the evangelical doctrine regarding states of perfection, we do need to state that marriage — full conjugal and family life of today — in spite of not representing an objective state of perfection according to the Gospel, nevertheless subjectively demands a much greater moral perfection from those who enter it; it does demand an increased effort towards reaching and preserving the moral perfection than ever before. This fact confirms once again the need for a re-education in the propaedeutic of the sacrament of marriage and the need for communities whose members — when deciding to marry — will be fully aware of how much this decision will demand from them in life from a moral point of view.

This seems to be the only proper approach to the problem. We could even admit to ourselves that Providence compels us in this direction. Therefore, we must raise the standards for ourselves.

The proposal to raise requirements is set to encounter human resistance. Then we cannot do anything else but calmly and thoroughly rethink the whole matter from the start. A Christian person needs to reconsider it in light of the mystery of the Incarnation — after all, this is the mystery of which the celebration, Christmas — opened all the opportunities for the above reflections on marriage and family. In such thorough reflection on these topics, under the light of the mystery of the Incarnation, one can find the answers and all the doubts will slowly disappear. This mystery is indeed not only divine but also human: it confirms all human qualities — that is to say confronts them in their depth — in a dimension of the person, grace, and sacrament. The Incarnation did not take place as a form of accusation of humanity but rather its justification, or as a way to pull it out of the original devaluation and weakness that humans defer to so often. We must not only take advantage of the light that rises from this mystery but also of the power that it contains and which never runs out.

# Unpacking the Text

Isn't it amazing what depth St. John Paul II has? As was mentioned earlier, this text was written by Father Wojtyła in 1957. In this letter, he takes the Nativity of Our Lord to reflect upon the Incarnation and uses this reflection to deepen our understanding of marriage. St. John Paul II begins this explanation of the Incarnation under the subtitle '*At the Foundations of Personalism,*' which he divides into three orders: the order of the person, the order of grace, and the order of the sacrament.

In '*The Order of Person,*' he explains the uniquely Christian distinction of *personalism*. It was only in understanding the Incarnation and the two natures of the Second Person of the Holy Trinity that the Fathers of the Church distinguished what it means to be a person. The concept of personhood began to be understood as "a being spiritually individualized and free" and this "spiritual dimension of reason and freedom belongs exclusively to the person."[66] This prepared the way for the eventual understanding of man as a person. Although there remains a great distance between the divine person and the human person, this personhood reveals a "fundamental link" between God and man.[67] Therefore, he says, the Incarnation holds the source of the identity of all humanity.

---

[66] *Reflections on Marriage, The Order of Person.*
[67] *Ibid.*

Within '*The Order of Grace*' section, St. John Paul II affirms that grace brings man closer to God. Because closeness to God can be understood as holiness, we can therefore say that *grace sanctifies*. It does so "by infusing the nature of the soul and its faculties with the elements of God's life."[68] With this gift of grace, the human person can live a new spiritual life, a *supernatural life*. Yet, the degree to which he lives within this supernatural life *is dependent upon man actualizing the sources of grace*. In other words, through the sacraments, God has given us the potential for this supernatural life of grace, but it is up to us to open ourselves to receive it. How open we are to grace becoming real in our lives determines our holiness, that is, our closeness to God.

He then takes this idea into the realm of marriage. He speaks of *conjugal spirituality*.[69] He affirms that the depth of a husband and wife's conjugal spirituality will depend on their openness to the actualization of grace in their shared, sacramental life: "(t)he degree of actualization of the supernatural forces in people united in marriage determines the sanctity of their union and their proximity to God."[70] Married couples will find closeness to God in direct correlation with how well their union can reflect, and find its true meaning within, the Communion of Divine Persons of the Holy Trinity. This Communion of Divine Persons

---

[68] *Ibid, The Order of Grace.*
[69] For context, he later describes conjugal spirituality as the couple's relationship with God. This is not their individual, personal relationships with God but an additional, special relationship with God they have in their unity.
[70] *Ibid.*

is the archetype of the loving union that each marriage is called to imitate. The married couple has a unique relationship to God because of the similarity of this *communion of love,* which is due to the grace that has been poured into their life through the mystery of the Incarnation.

In *'The Order of Sacrament,'* he teaches that it was through the event of the Incarnation that God entered into humanity in a profound way. The Incarnation touches every part of humanity including the body, and it is precisely the body of the Man-God, Jesus Christ, that becomes "a visible sign and a prototype of all such signs."[71] Through participation in each of the sacraments, man participates in the mystery of the Incarnation, in a life wholly supernatural; and not only participates, but "lengthens and extends" it.[72] In each sacrament, the efficacious sign of grace makes possible the fullness of human life as God intended it. Yet, participation in the sacraments alone does not bring this life to completion; it is left to each human person to pull out from the supernatural gifts all that it contains so that he might enter into this life of grace.

For the sacrament of marriage, he says, "there are simultaneously two persons that enter the orbit of grace."[73] In understanding that the spouses themselves are the ministers of the sacrament of marriage, each spouse has a responsibility to the other to give of themselves in love and enter into this orbit of grace.

---

[71] *Ibid, The Order of Sacrament.*
[72] *Ibid.*
[73] *Ibid.*

Only when both spouses open themselves to God and all that the supernatural gift of grace has to offer can the authentic sacrament of marriage come to fruition. They become conduits of this grace for each other: "(t)hese two persons are for each other direct instruments of the action of God"[74] in their married life. (*How amazing is this!*)

Fr. Kwiatkowski, who brought these texts back to the public's view, reflects further, that this "Reflections on Marriage" text demonstrates how Trinitarian love is rendered visible in the daily life of husband and wife. There is a wholly permeating communion between the man and the woman in marriage, and this is the reflection of the loving union within the Trinity. The focus in this text is the particular actualization of this profound truth in the daily life of marriage. The conjugal spirituality is "one spirituality lived by two, where both spouses enter the orbit of grace and traveling the same path each with his/her own steps, they become for each other the instruments of the action of God."[75] *Their marriage as a union becomes a supernatural life.*

In *Education for Marriage—the Culture of the Person*, he begins by recognizing that the we should focus on the *person* to understand marriage.[76] Marriage is a

---

[74] *Ibid.*

[75] *Grygiel*, 18, "È una spiritualità vissuta in due, dove entrambi gli sposi entrano nell'orbita della grazia e percorrendo con i propri passi lo stesso cammino, diventano l'uno per l'altro gli instrumenti dell'agire di Dio."

[76] *Reflections on Marriage*, 2. *Education for Marriage — the Culture of the Person.*

joining of two human *persons*, and it is not merely a bonding because of sexual attraction or amiability. While the psychological, sociological, and physiological elements do play a part in the natural union of man and woman, none of these sciences can reach the core of the nature of human love. He states that "man in his totality is a person, and love, as an act of a man—seen integrally and profoundly—is always an act of a person."[77] Each of the other sciences fall short in seeing man as an integral whole. While marriage preparation ought naturally to include all that has to do with communication, relationships, and sexuality, which would include a variety of other sciences, "all these elements must be then integrated by submitting them to the person, to the man in his totality."[78]

Ethics should guide marriage preparation. What is most important, he reiterates, is that man is seen as an integral whole. In teaching the ethics of marriage, we must always see man in two moments: "*who he is* and *who he ought to be*."[79] This total vision of man must permeate all that is being taught. This personalistic point of view keeps the other sciences from taking the education in a too one-sided direction or even from undermining it. This is because, he says, "marriage demands, above all, the culture of the person."[80] All that the couple must learn, including sexual love, must rise to the dignity of the human person. It is the "vision

---

[77] *Ibid.*
[78] *Ibid.*
[79] *Ibid.*
[80] *Ibid.*

of the person"[81] that must illuminate all preparation for the married life to which the engaged couple aspire. Whatever we teach engaged couples, we must meet them where they are (*who man is*) in the realness of their life. We cannot rush the spiritual journey that each individual takes. Yet, we also do not just say "such is life" and leave them there. We must still point each couple to God's vision for their life (*who man ought to be*).[82]

St. John Paul II further explains that, in a general sense, normally it would be the function or responsibility of the society to prepare couples for marriage. However, when society has lost its sense of the dignity and vision of the person, it is incapable of the task: "when the culture of the person diminishes in the society ... there are no means for the propaedeutic of marriage other than creating communities in which the culture of a person can grow."[83] While these created communities to support the culture of the person will have their challenges, we must make this truth heard to all of society: "the future of marriage, the future of all and each individual marriage, depends on each and every one of us, on the level of culture of the person in all of us."[84] This is most important when preparing for the sacrament of marriage.

In a Christian society, St. John Paul II explains, the preparation for marriage and for the sacrament of

---

[81] *Ibid.*

[82] We have seen this in part 1, which we called the tension between the Real and the Ideal.

[83] *Ibid.*

[84] *Ibid.*

marriage would be mostly the same. However, the distinction between the two is found in the mystery of the Incarnation, which imparts an even greater value of the person. When a Christian community sees that the wider society no longer upholds the dignity of the person, it is up to the Christian community to re-educate and bring these truths into culture once again: "It would become a sort of re-education in the field of the sacrament of marriage."[85]

Marriage preparation is more than a list of instructions to be understood; we must create a new community that supports the culture of the person where the couples can learn and grow. The preparation and education of marriage becomes then a task of the entire community and not just of an instructor. We can see how his experience with the *Środowisko* community shapes his understanding here.

We can also see how the community he later initiated with The Rule would fit this need. It would seem that a committed group of married couples with the purpose of prayer, spiritual growth, apostolate, and the continued education in the truth of marriage and family would fit this community needed to nurture the preparation of marriage. He leaves the concrete details open but reaffirms the importance that it must uphold the culture of the person:

> This culture (of the person) is born on such vision of the person, his being, his capabilities and his destiny that can be found in the content and

---

[85] *Ibid.*

objective dynamic of the mystery of the Incarnation.[86]

In his final section of the *Reflections on Marriage*, St. John Paul II speaks about *Economy and Personalism*. The profound economic changes in modern society have made authentically living out the vocation of marriage and family difficult. He highlights a few of the real problems: the need for both spouses to have professional jobs and the consequences this has on family life, the lack of sufficient funds to care for one's family, and the lack of adequate housing in which to properly raise a family in the truth of the Gospel. *The "spiritual ideal"[87] of a Christian community and high morality that this requires will not come naturally in the modern world, he says, but must be established.*

The mode in which Christians had lived will no longer suffice in this modern society:

> The changed socioeconomic conditions simply require an even higher culture of the person so that the marriage and family could live on moral levels necessary for their human and Christian character.[88]

Christian society has been surprised by the radical changes in the world, and not having been prepared to respond, he explained, they have seen a decline in the morality of marriages and families. (*Remember this was written more than sixty years ago. How much more of a*

---

[86] *Ibid.*

[87] *Ibid.*, 3. *Economy and Personalism.*

[88] *Ibid.*

*decline have we seen since then!?*) To live as a Christian in our modern world demands a certain heroism. He states:

> Certainly, in ordinary conditions, men cannot be obliged to heroism, but there are certain extraordinary conditions that may demand it of him.[89]

We must recognize, he says, that spouses striving to live within the culture of the person in our modern world will only succeed with extraordinary strength and commitment to the truth. Knowing this reality, we must find a way to weave it into marriage preparation. Within our society, an authentically Christian marriage:

> Subjectively demands a much greater moral perfection from those who enter it; it does demand an increased effort towards reaching and preserving the moral perfection than ever before.[90]

Marriage preparation must re-educate the Christian community being sure engaged couples understand the demanding task before them.

St. John Paul II concludes his reflection referring back to the mystery of the Incarnation that has changed and heightened every aspect of what it means to be human. The graces to be born into this new life are available through the sacraments, and these same

---

[89] *Ibid.*
[90] *Ibid.*

graces give one the strength to fight against the temptation to weakness:

> We must not only take advantage of the light that rises from this mystery but also of the power that it contains, and which never runs out.[91]

---

[91] *Ibid.*

# 9

# "Love is the Moral Foundation of Marriage"[92]

## Synopsis

The second accompanying text was written by Bishop Karol Wojtyła in 1961 when he was auxiliary bishop of Kraków. It is a reflection on marriage, which he continually affirms is based on the pastoral experience he has had with married couples in their concrete, daily struggles of life. St. John Paul II introduces the reflection noting the multitude of social and economic changes as well as cultural and ideological ones that are occurring in society. Because of this, he states, we need a new way to understand and describe marriage: "a new model of marriage."[93]

---

[92] K. WOJTYŁA, *Miłość jest moralnym fundamentum małżeństwa. Artykuł opublikowany przez biskupa Karola Wojtyłę w* "Przewodniku katolickim" w 1961 roku, in , in K. WOJTYŁA, Teksty poznańskie [the texts of Poznań], edited by M. Jędraszewski, Wydawnicto św. Wojciecha, Poznań 1997, 47-56. Translated by A. Pata, 2020.
[93] *Love is the Moral Foundation of Marriage,* introductory paragraphs.

His attempt will not be to repeat already understood themes of marriage, but to "make theology encounter experience."[94] Knowing marriage is a sacrament, he recognizes that reason alone will not achieve its full understanding but that we must find our answers also through Divine Revelation.

---

[94] *Ibid.*

# LOVE IS THE MORAL FOUNDATION OF MARRIAGE - BY BISHOP KAROL WOJTYŁA[95]

## The state of today's marriage[96]

When speaking about the state of today's Catholic marriage, what immediately comes to one's mind is the changed socio-economic relations, and, in some ways, also cultural and ideological, which have been shaping a certain new model of marriage. If we wish to analyze this model from within, we must begin with some theological principles. Understanding that marriage is a sacrament, we are right to admit that it is impossible to get its clear vision through a mere rational analysis, or fully comprehend it without acknowledging the premises of Revelation or the supernatural element that they contain. Without acknowledging this element, it is also impossible to draw a new model of marriage, even though its new foundations seem to do just that through the socio-economic factors.

---

[95] K. WOJTYŁA, *Miłość jest moralnym fundamentum małżeństwa. Artykuł opublikowany przez biskupa Karola Wojtyłę w* "Przewodniku katolickim" w 1961 roku, in , in K. WOJTYŁA, Teksty poznańskie [the texts of Poznań], edited by M. Jędraszewski, Wydawnicto św. Wojciecha, Poznań 1997, 47-56. Translated by A. Pata, 2020.

[96] *Note bene:* the Polish title from the previous note reads: "*Love is the moral foundation of marriage. Article published by bishop Karol Wojtyla in the "Catholic Guide" in 1961.*" However, in the archival texts, we find the title of this section of text as "*the state of today's marriage.*" We've included both titles to reflect this.

I am not going to repeat well known facts. But I want to try to extract from the sources and theological premises all that, in my opinion, could be relevant to understand, and, above all, to shape in a practical way the model of marriage that we clearly see forming today. It will be an attempt to make theology encounter experience.

### 1. Be Perfect

To that effect I would like to make a reference to certain theses from theological teaching on Christian perfection. According to the words of St Matthew: "Therefore you will be perfect, just as your Father in Heaven is perfect" (MT 5,48). We stand by the statement that there is a recommendation, or even obligation, to pursue perfection, which is *universal*, and the road to its realization is indicated by the commandment of love. We actualize the perfection of Christian life by fulfilling the commandment of love. The more we fulfill it, the more fully we actualize this perfection that is discussed in the Gospel. The commandment of love itself is also universal, which once again confirms the universal character of the call to perfection. However, there are different ways to its actualization, just like there are different vocations and different directions in life of different people, and, therefore, also different ways of observing the commandment of love. Love itself, that is the subject of the commandment, is a theological virtue, a divine virtue, which explains its internal power to unite man with God, while remaining, at the same time, the most beautiful, moral way of a person relating to another person. These two elements: supernatural, therefore theological, and personalistic (personal), make up for the content of this "greatest commandment," and they outline the entire character of the Christian perfection.

### 2. State of Perfection

There is another question that is connected with the aforementioned teaching on the perfection of Christian life and that is the question of the so-called state of perfection. We do not mean here the internal spiritual state, which has already reached perfection based on love, but rather a specific social formation, a certain system of communal or solitary life, which is particularly favorable to reaching the perfection described in the Gospel. At the basis of this state there are three main evangelical counsels that a person promises to observe through a vow of chastity, poverty, and obedience. The result of these vows is a state (meaning a system of human life) — the one that we call "religious." (By the way, the so-called secular institutions are where we find the most modern form of a religious order. Secularism does not disturb its spirit, even though it would disturb participation in priesthood. Priesthood and religious order are clearly two distinct formations).

### 3. The Married State of Life

In light of all that has been said above, it is easy to establish that marriage, as a state, does not identify itself with the "state of perfection." (A marriage is, of course, a certain state that is a well-defined formation of human life with its own specific structure.) Well, the structure of a marriage is not such that everything in it must be oriented toward the realization of the ideal of Christian perfection, as it is in the case of a religious order. Nevertheless, *the married state of life certainly does not exclude Christian perfection*, and if we take into consideration this special supernatural endowment that spouses get equipped with through the *sacrament of marriage*, then the previously used statement "does not exclude Christian perfection" seems maybe quite conservative, as it is too negative. In fact, the perfection of Christian life is based on that supernatural endowment that we owe to the holy sacraments (and so also to marriage). Of course, it does not end here — this perfection requires appropriate conditions — and this is where the meaning of "state" according to the above referred concept comes to full light.

Marriage is not such a "state" (of perfection). Spouses begin their new life with a certain supernatural endowment in which there is also a full-fledged possibility of realizing Christian perfection, but their "state" itself does not help them in this anymore or does not dispose them to it. (Maybe this expression is too pessimistic; instead let's say then that their state doesn't orient them specifically toward it). Catholic theology does not remove marriage from the supernatural orientation. But it is not convinced about its orientation towards perfection of the married state of life itself. How can we explain this idea? Clearly by the fact that such orientation involves realization of evangelic counsels, and each one of them refers to what is "better and nonmandatory". However, it is not the same as the actual possibility of realization of Christian perfection in sacramental marriage, and here the perspectives are clear, as they arise from the mere idea of marriage. A union of two people that is based on love creates some distinct possibilities to fulfill this commandment, the "greatest" one, the one that perfection really depends on.

### 4. *Christian Perfection in Marriage*

Why are we talking about all of this? Because it looks like the teaching on perfection has been slightly obscured by the teaching on the state of perfection, which led to a certain almost programmed minimalism in regards to marriage. Marriage is a respected institution, maybe even glorified in theory — "in theory," as this respect and glorification apply more to God's idea of marriage, and rightfully so. Meanwhile, when the idea needs to turn into reality, then the image gets obscured. What is the reason? In part, the reason is undoubtedly in some facts. We are met with diverse sins of the spouses, which in the confessional of the confessor cost so much that he even calls them his "cross." (Maybe they are also the cross of spouses. It is worth considering.)

But there is also a second reason to this attitude. Within us there is probably a kind of prejudice related to the question of flesh, some trace of Manichaeism, which doesn't allow us to imagine reaching perfection (spiritual and supernatural) in the state where the questions of flesh are such an important, such an essential factor of a united life of two people. The textbooks on Christian perfection are silent on this subject, and, in general, they give methods for perfection adapting to the conditions that exist in the "state of perfection." What is Christian perfection supposed to look like in the realization of other people, especially spouses who became "two in one flesh?" It turns out that we link holiness to the divine idea of marriage, but we do not demand it from the married people, nor do we work in that direction. The suggestion that marriage should instead be treated "from the side of sin" is so strong and so overwhelming that few people think to treat it "in terms of perfection." We are not equipped for it mentally; we also lack conviction.

### 5. Need to Get Out of the "Dead End"

All the while, through life in practice and the experiences that it brings, arises a reflection that this may be the right and really the only way to break this "dead end" that has been created around marriage. It is identified by facts, by press articles, ample publications, and, besides all that, by a growing "lifestyle," which forces itself always more into the customs of the believers, not only those Christians solely by name, and, more often than ever, gets accepted as something "normal." For this purpose, I have gathered several commentaries by publicists. Well, our experience also says that marriage has for the believer, in many cases, the character of a test of spiritual and moral strength, the strength of faith and Christian character. Social customs and traditions of the community seem to help less and less. It is important then that we all—the faithful and the pastors—do not get overwhelmed by the significance of the numerous facts. If we are to keep our faith in marriage as God's matter—as one of the areas where what plays the role is not only a man with his concupiscence and his flawed nature, but also God with His grace—we must not only assume a strong conviction about the possibilities of perfection in that state but also make the effort to put them in practice.

Why is this our way out of the "dead end?" First and foremost because marriage, based on my pastoral experience, can be maintained on the level that we could call "natural" (i.e., according to the requirements of laws of nature, the natural moral order) only on the condition of striving towards perfection. However, it will not remain on this level when there is a clear assumption of some negative norm, of just some kind of "not allowed."

*6. "Fidelity to Nature" or "Fidelity to Grace?"*

The non-Catholic party presents a program of conscious parenthood. It suggests loudly all the suggestions for contraception without any limitations. We cannot accept this position even though the sole idea of conscious parenthood is acceptable on our end. It is all about the model of conjugal morality that stands behind it. This is where we find the sensitive point of this entire question which lays in the vision of a marriage rather than procreation itself.

And maybe this is why it is not enough to highlight solely the fidelity to nature ("marriage faithful to nature"). Theoretically, this expression is correct but this simple and easy "fidelity to nature" (especially in the way most happen to comprehend it) conflicts with the system of conditions that we already know and doesn't fit in the "new model." The simple and uncomplicated fidelity to nature would mean a number of children often exceeding the strength of today's overworked mothers, and of fathers struggling to earn enough to meet the needs of the family — here, we also need to listen to their voices as they do not say it without reason. And if one puts forward the postulate of fidelity to nature within the framework of conscious parenthood, we must realize that the "fidelity to nature" alone is not enough.

If the spouses, following fidelity to nature, *are to practice abstinence*, even if only periodically, then *fidelity to grace* must be brought to the fore. This clearly delineates an interior tension of the whole problem. As much as the moral expectations of the Church toward married couples refer essentially to the "fidelity to nature," on the level of the fallen nature they become hard to accept and even more difficult to realize. Moreover, when thrown in the form of a pure ban, they only provoke opposition and misunderstanding. They need to be presented differently so they can be received in a different way. It seems that conjugal abstinence (even only temporary) is difficult to practice if it isn't supported by certain, even modest, pursuit of perfection available in marriage, by even modest asceticism in life and relationship. If we don't assume such position, our entire program will always continue to create misunderstandings and be limited to the very superficial controversy on "Why does the Church allow one method of contraception and will not allow the other ones?"

Inside this whole question there is a moment that I would dare to call "dramatic." It may seem like in the whole structure of conjugal life, sin, and perfection somehow run side by side, and the boundary line between them is very thin. However, this is thoroughly an illusion. A couple consciously living in fidelity to nature compared to a couple living in sin is not only different by the fact that one practices Holt's method[97] and the other one uses contraceptives. Instead, there is a very profound difference in approach to life: on one end there is a certain effort— that I will not hesitate calling ascetic, on the other hand there is abandoning everything to the effects of spontaneous impulses and trends coming from the environment.

### 7. The Sacramental Grace Is Not Just a Theory

We must clearly recognize that sacramental grace of marriage is not just some theory but a real endowment from which spouses can, and should, build a certain Christian perfection pertinent to their vocation and the multilateral totality that is their conjugal life. I would not hesitate to say that the past times have proven this truth; admittedly through rather negative examples, through the way of contrast, but they did expose it, nevertheless. Today, if we want to avoid any misunderstandings, somewhat against the reality of the facts but, equally, also thanks to them, we must think of conjugal life more in the categories of Christian perfection. The spouses must be aware why these burdens are placed on their shoulders that are often so hard to carry. Only Christ has the right to impose crosses as He Himself carried the weight of one—in the framework of fidelity to nature they become hard to comprehend and it is a natural impulse that one tries to free oneself from them.

Christian perfection consists in love. Love is also the moral foundation of marriage. Therefore, marriage

---

[97] Dr. Jan Holt, a Dutch Physician, was known for his "Holt temperature method" explained in his book *Marriage and Periodic Abstinence*, 1963.

opens up the possibility of Christian perfection. While Manichaeism and Puritanism decipher ethical and ascetical problems following the border line between "matters of flesh" and "matters of soul," the Gospel pushes us to decipher these problems in another way: "what is love (also in matters of the flesh) and what is not." What is love is also perfection, even when it takes place in the areas of the flesh, and what is not love is not perfection even if it has a very spiritual character.

We can agree that what is not love tends to assume "on the side" the identity of love, and this is why we are so often met with "what isn't love." Here it is important to reflect well on what is the cause and what is the effect. Is it easy to find imperfection and sin in marriage because it is simply a "state of imperfection"? Or is it the opposite — marriage is imperfect and sinful because we stopped associating it with the idea and the possibility of perfection?

There is one more question here. We must not allow a conviction in the minds, and especially in the will of the spouses, of the hopelessness of their moral situation within the framework of Catholic ethics. Yet, this is what often takes place — spouses born in certain generations and whose conjugal life is particularly intensive sometimes do not come to the confessional for many years. Their sins are not born within an internal isolation but are also born of various other deficiencies in moral and religious life which need to be filled first, for the sin to disappear.

### 8. In Line With Reality

What is the point of all these reflections and thoughts? The main point is to bring out the certain truth about marriage. Modern man finds himself often in front of this one essential challenge: You impose an unbearable burden on me, and at the same time, you contrast it with this "state of perfection" in which, who knows, maybe it is easier to live (obviously, this argumentation is limping but at the same time it is very much on the scale of man). First and foremost, this matter must be presented in a way that is truthful. This brings a question whether our entire way of thinking about marriage is not "too low" with simultaneous high demands on it. Maybe it is best to pose the question entirely on a higher level: presume more to be able to demand more (just as much as we need). But then we must also prepare ourselves more and assist more.

Most of all, it is necessary to present these questions in line with the truth and according to reality because, after all, the truth always has a great future ahead of it.

# Unpacking the Text

We now approach the second accompanying text. Still with us? Wonderful! We realize that these texts are profound. Several books could probably be written on the depth of what St. John Paul II is saying here. However, for now, we will walk through the writing and use it to expound upon The Rule, so we can fully understand St. John Paul II's intentions therein.

This second text was written in 1961 when St. John Paul II was auxiliary bishop of Kraków. It is a reflection on marriage, which he continually affirms is based on the pastoral experience he has had with married couples in their concrete, daily struggles of life. You will recognize that we've seen this before. He always emphasizes this Real and Ideal tension, or what he calls the "integral vision of the person." Seeing each person always in two instances: who he or she is and who they are meant to be. St. John Paul II introduces the reflection noting the multitude of social and economic changes as well as cultural and ideological ones occurring in society. Because of this, he states, we need a new way to understand and describe marriage: "a new model of marriage."[98] His attempt will not be to repeat already understood themes of marriage, but to "make theology encounter experience."[99] Knowing marriage is a sacrament, he recognizes that reason alone will not achieve its full understanding, but that

---

[98] *Love is the Moral Foundation of Marriage,* introductory paragraphs.
[99] *Ibid.*

we must find our answers also through Divine Revelation.

He has eight subsections to this piece.

*Be Perfect*: In the first section, St. John Paul II draws our attention to the Gospel of Matthew when Jesus says, "Be you therefore perfect as your heavenly Father is perfect" (Mt 5:48). He sees this as a universal call to holiness and perfection. This calling to perfection, he says, can only be realized through Christ's commandment of love, which is not given to just a chosen few. We must recognize that there is a universal character to the call to perfection.[100] How this commandment of love is lived out in different lives depends upon their own personal vocation. He explains that love is a theological virtue that binds the inner soul to God. This love of the soul to God, he explains, does seem more morally beautiful than that love between two people. Yet these two elements, theological and personalistic, are present in the commandment to love and they designate "the entire character of the Christian perfection."[101]

*State of Perfection*: He moves on to explain the *State of Perfection* as it had been understood in Christian thought. A state of perfection does not guarantee a person will reach perfection in this state nor assume that one who enters such a state would already have reached perfection. It means that this state in life is directed toward perfection. The life of a religious who

---

[100] *Love is the Moral Foundation of Marriage, 1. Be Perfect.*
[101] *Ibid.*

has taken the vows of chastity, poverty, and obedience lives within a state, or system of life, "which is particularly favorable to reaching the perfection described in Gospel."[102] This label of 'state of perfection' would exclude all those who did not take strict vows to the evangelical counsels.

*The Married State of Life*: The third section affirms that based on the previous explanation, as a 'state of life,' marriage would not be considered a 'state of perfection.' This is true because unlike the religious state, marriage in its basic structure does not necessarily predispose the couple towards holiness or Christian perfection. However, St. John Paul II explains "the married state of life certainly does not exclude Christian perfection,"[103] especially considering the grace the couple receives from the sacrament. In fact, in light of "this special supernatural endowment" from the Sacrament of Marriage, he reflects that the previous statement is perhaps too negative. In fact, "(s)pouses begin their new life with a certain supernatural endowment, in which there is also a full-fledged possibility of realizing Christian perfection,"[104] even without the help of a predisposition to a certain state. Although marriage would be excluded from a state of perfection by the terms our Christian tradition have given us, St. John Paul II insists that the "union of two people that is based on love creates some distinct possibilities to fulfill this commandment, the 'greatest' one, the one

---

[102] *Ibid.*, 2. *State of Perfection.*
[103] *Ibid.*, 3. *The Married State of Life.*
[104] *Ibid.*

that perfection really depends on."[105] Spouses can find holiness (Christian perfection), through their marriage.

*Christian Perfection in Marriage*: The next section reflects on why St. John Paul II has chosen to examine marriage in this way. The traditional understandings of states of life and the exclusion of marriage from a state of perfection has, he explains, encoded into our thinking a sort of minimalism when it comes to marriage and the Christian walk of holiness. While often marriage is exulted when spoken in biblical reference to God's love toward human persons, many have had difficulty bringing this higher vision of marriage into the reality of a particular husband and wife with all their unique challenges. Nevertheless, the ideal must be brought into reality. He suggests perhaps what makes this task especially difficult is the challenge of there being so many different personalities of couples, each with their own temptations. Another issue he raises as to why it is difficult to bring the idea to reality is that there has been "a kind of prejudice related to the question of flesh, some trace of Manichaeism."[106] Some consider the spirit higher than the body and could not perceive of anything being holy that would so precisely involve the body, such as the sexuality of husband and wife. We have limited our idea of marriage, he says, by treating it almost on the side of sin and not demanding holiness of the couples in their daily life. He admits that, at the time of his writing this text, the

---

[105] *Ibid.*
[106] *Ibid.*, 4. *Christian Perfection in Marriage.*

understanding of marriage as a possible way to holiness was deeply lacking in marriage preparation.

*Need to Get Out of the 'Dead End*: St. John Paul II begins to explain a way out of this negative view on marriage in the next section. Marriage is being hemmed in on all sides in modern society. In addition to the minimalistic view of marriage from an older understanding, contemporary culture's view on marriage is shifting constantly. He cautions against allowing one's faith to be "overwhelmed by the significance of the numerous facts"[107] and the press articles that attempt to recreate the definition of marriage. (*Remember, he wrote this in 1961; yet, how true this is today! Perhaps, to even a greater degree...*) If we want to believe in marriage as a sacred institution, created by God, that with the help of God's grace can lead a couple to holiness, he says, "We must not only assume a strong conviction about the possibilities of perfection in that state but also make the effort to put them in practice."[108] He believes this to be the case based on the experience he has witnessed and explains that striving for holiness and Christian perfection in marriage is the only way out of this "dead end."

*'Fidelity to Nature' or 'Fidelity to Grace'?*: This next section presents a discussion on how the conversation about family planning and contraception should be improved. (*This is an important section for seeing the Real and the Ideal in a particular situation while also understanding the teaching of* Humanae Vitae *that would*

---

[107] *Ibid.,* 5. *Need to Get Out of the "Dead End."*
[108] *Ibid.*

be proclaimed seven years **after** this piece was written.) St. John Paul II explains that we cannot accept the non-Catholic view of allowing all contraceptive options. It is not because we do not agree with the idea that a married couple ought to be free to discern their family size but because of the inherent conjugal morality that lies behind such thinking. Here he explains that it is not enough to merely assert natural law and demand married couples to be faithful to nature. Although the argument is correct, it falls on deaf ears because it fails to address the multifaceted situations in which couples find themselves. The people will hear it only as insensitive to the needs of real life. Explaining again from experience, he notes that total fidelity to nature would produce extremely large families, and with the shifting socioeconomic culture, many parents find this a legitimate strain. Doing this:

> Would mean a number of children often exceeding the strength of today's overworked mothers, and of fathers struggling to earn enough to meet the needs of the family — here, we also need to listen to their voices as they do not say it without reason.[109]

This fidelity to nature is not enough for this new understanding of marriage in order to contest with modern ideology.

When couples must practice periodic abstinence, they need faithfulness to grace more than only to nature. St. John Paul II emphasizes that this is where the tension lies. The Church is right in speaking of

---

[109] *Ibid.*, 6. *"Fidelity to Nature" or Fidelity to Grace"?*

fidelity to nature, but when a couple is faced with practicing periodic abstinence, this is not enough. Such a teaching is difficult to accept and live out in man's fallen nature; they need fidelity to grace. He also explains that a simple ban against contraception, without an explanation as to why only incites misunderstandings and opposition. He says, "It seems that conjugal abstinence (even only temporary) is difficult to practice if it isn't supported by certain, even modest, pursuit of perfection available in marriage."[110] A couple will not be able to joyfully live out authentic Christian marriage without striving for holiness and Christian perfection as a couple, which in other texts Wojtyła named conjugal spirituality. Finally, he urges the listener to reject the notion that the line between sin and holiness in marriage seems very thin. The couple that chooses to walk the way of holiness have oriented their lives in faith, while others live by impulses and the shifting principles of modern culture. There is a great distance between the two orientations.

*The Sacramental Grace Is Not Just a Theory*: The seventh subsection focuses in on the supernatural endowment of sacramental grace in marriage as the key element to be able to achieve Christian perfection in marriage. The new model for understanding marriage must focus on the spouses' vocation toward Christian perfection, St. John Paul II says. In this way, the married couple who chooses to follow the teaching of the Church on difficult issues, such as contraception, would find strength in the meaning of their vocation and learn to call upon sacramental grace: "The spouses

---

[110] *Ibid.*

must be aware why these burdens are placed on their shoulders that are often so hard to carry."[111] Only through our Christianity can we understand marriage: "Only Christ has the right to impose crosses as He Himself carried the weight of one."[112] Without this view and only in light of natural law arguments, the burden seems incomprehensible and one would work to be freed from it. He explains that because Christian perfection is formed by love and love is also the moral basis of marriage, then "marriage opens up the possibility of Christian perfection."[113] To those who would postulate that the things of the spirit are higher than that of the flesh, he points them to see all these things through the light of the Gospel, which focuses on love. He says, "What is love is also perfection, even when it takes place in the areas of the flesh."[114] The opposite also being true: things that are not love, even if they have a spiritual looking exterior, are not perfection. He asks his listeners to ask themselves which is the cause and which the effect: are sin and moral failings so frequently found in marriages because it is a so-called state of imperfection, or are they found because in this negative view of marriage, we have lowered our expectations and not called them to the true purpose of their vocation in Christian perfection? (*It is a difficult but necessary question for us all, especially those in marriage ministry. Have we lowered the bar, thinking that we are helping when in reality, as St. John Paul II has shown us, this is taking away what can help*

---

[111] *Ibid. 7. The Sacramental Grace Is Not Just a Theory.*
[112] *Ibid.*
[113] *Ibid.*
[114] *Ibid.*

*their marriage succeed: the pursuit of holiness? This definitely gives us something to ponder.*)

*In Line with Reality*: This is the eighth and final subsection of this reflection. He concludes his thoughts by explaining that we must get to the truth about marriage and bring theories into the real lives of ordinary spouses. We must change our lens of how we view marriage. If our view remains at a basic level and we do not give the spouses much to aim for, the burdens we are asking of them will be too great indeed. Instead, "presume more to be able to demand more (just as much as we need)."[115] When couples have a reason to reach for holiness, the burdens will be more easily born. He affirms that marriage preparation must be organized to explain this and give a greater help to engaged couples.

---

[115] *Ibid., 8. In Line with Reality.*

# A Note About the Following Chapters

Now, we bring the focus back to The Rule. There was so much wisdom packed into these two documents! To help us better dive into what it means to live The Rule, we have gathered the wisdom scattered throughout these documents and organized it as it pertains to each of the themes included in The Rule: Community, 'The Real and the Ideal', *Humanae Vitae*, Marriage Unity, Christian Morality, Conjugal Spirituality, Studying Marriage, Apostolate, and Prayer.

In doing so, we hope to more clearly comprehend St. John Paul II's vision for the Married Couple Groups living by The Rule. St. John Paul II's Rule holds the key to entering more deeply into divine love and unlocking lasting joy. May God open our minds and our hearts to allow Christ's self-giving love for His bride to permeate our own marriages, and draw us deeper into the heart of the Father. As St. John Paul II said, we pray for each couple that "the integral teachings of Jesus Christ on marriage and family, proclaimed by the Church, could be accomplished in their married life with full understanding and full love."[116]

---

[116] *The Rule*, 4.

# 10

## COMMUNITY AND COMMITMENT
## THE RULE, #1, #6

Writing The Rule itself affirmed the need for community. The Rule isn't for couples to pray through on their own; it is to form Married Couple *Groups*. We need each other if we are going to stand strong against the flood of secular culture. When we support each other, we are not alone, and the journey becomes a little easier. Together in Christ, we find our strength; we are lifted above the struggle.

Why is community necessary for joy? Can't a couple just take the basic themes from The Rule and implement them in their own marriage without joining any kind of group? According to St. John Paul II, they can't. They may try, but they would not have success in finding the lasting joy they seek. In this post-Christian age, they will be standing alone against a daily onslaught of other antithetical value systems and opinions. Would an army be successful sending troops one at a time into enemy lines? No. There is something to be said about strength in numbers.

The focus of this book is to understand The Rule and use these texts that are new to the English-speaking world (and therefore offer a unique, fresh light) to highlight what St. John Paul II intended for Married Couple Groups. We would be remiss, though, if we did not mention that you can find much on his explanation of persons as being *called to communion* and that this is a reflection of the Blessed Trinity, whom he calls a divine *Communion of Persons*. As much as we love all his rich teaching from his life and pontificate, we cannot go into all these aspects here. We encourage you to read his plentiful writings on all these topics. The scope of this book is limited to presenting The Rule.

## Living an authentically Christian marriage requires heroic virtue. To live heroic virtue requires community.

As we have seen from part 1, even fifty years ago the culture was opposed to the truth of marriage. Look at how much more hostile the culture is now. And this hostility is not just in respect to the teaching of *Humanae Vitae*, but the truth of marriage as proclaimed by Jesus Christ and taught by the Catholic Church — the lifelong covenant between one man and one woman. St. John Paul II affirms that it is more difficult to live out one's faith now than it was a few generations ago when the general culture more or less supported Christian morality. He said that how

Christians had lived will no longer be enough to sustain their Christianity in our modern world:

> It is truly more important to realize that the changed socioeconomic conditions simply require an *even higher culture of the person* so that the marriage and family could live on moral levels necessary for their human and Christian character.[117]

Living as a Christian in our contemporary world, St. John Paul II said, demands heroic virtue. At another point, he reiterates that living an authentically Christian marriage:

> ... Subjectively *demands a much greater moral perfection* from those who enter it; it does demand an increased effort towards reaching and preserving the moral perfection *than ever before.*[118]

If married couples need to have an even higher level of morality, how are they to sustain such virtue? He answers: through the support of an authentically Christian community.

Living at a level of heroic virtue on your own, even as a married couple, while perhaps possible, is difficult and spiritually exhausting. St. John Paul II knew that it could be made easier with the support of a Catholic community. The Rule itself, in addition to being a

---

[117] *Reflections on Marriage, 3. Economy and Personalism.* Emphasis added.
[118] *Ibid.* Emphasis added.

confirmation of the need for community, puts
community into action.

When we were first married, we felt a deep desire
to serve the Church in the area of marriage and family.
Instead of getting jobs and settling down, we decided
to move to Rome. *How grand this will be!* we thought.
We envisioned this romantic experience of living in
Italy as newlyweds and pioneering upon this great
religious desire. The reality was far from it. We got an
apartment in the outskirts of Rome and were
surrounded by lovely Italians. Yet, when no one
speaks your language, you feel isolated. We couldn't
easily contact anyone. Internet wasn't what it is today,
nor did Facebook and social networking exist. We had
different class schedules and were only seeing each
other like ships passing in the night. Getting used to
each other as spouses was intensified because we had
no one else to reach out to. Instead of living a way of
love, we began to count the costs.

Neither one of us could do anything right to the
other. Here we had traveled across the globe to serve
God, and we were rewashing the other's dishes or
refolding the socks because the other didn't do it right
and bickering about every little thing. We were driving
each other crazy. It was humbling but real, and we
realized a few things:

- That our spouse couldn't fulfill our needs;
  only God could do so. (You would think
  that would have been obvious, but these
  "prince charming" and "happily ever after"
  notions find their way into your thoughts.)

- That we needed friendship.

## If a community does not exist, it must be created.

Some fortunate people have such a community already around them. However, at times even among Christian communities (and especially modern society as a whole), St. John Paul II says there has arisen a loss of the understanding of the dignity and integral vision of the person. He says a community must uphold the dignity of the person and see each person in those two moments: who they are and who they are meant to be. This is what he calls the integral vision of the person. We need a community able to meet a person in that realness, sympathize with their struggles and challenges, and truly hear them. At the same time, this community must call them to holiness and show them the greatness of their vocation. If such a community is lacking, it is necessary then to form a community that upholds the culture of the person:

> ... When the culture of the person diminishes in the society ... there are no means for the propaedeutic of marriage other than creating communities in which the culture of a person can grow.[119]

The community provides the environment in which the newly married couple finds faith-filled friendship and support. It ought to be an environment where

---

[119] *Ibid., 2. Education for Marriage – the Culture of the Person.*

couples can learn and grow. In fact, St. John Paul II asserts that the responsibility of forming and preparing couples for marriage is not just the job of marriage catechists but the responsibility of the entire community. His experience with the *Środowisko* community undoubtedly affirmed this.[120]

Sam, a husband from a WCI Married Couple Group shares:

> After nearly a year of meeting with the other couples in our Married Couples Group, my work required me to be away from it for a couple of months. While I continued to pray for the group, the other couples, and their families, the loss was difficult. Not only did I miss the sharing, discussion, friendship and support of that faith-filled Christian community, but I also began to feel the distance in my own marriage.
>
> Though I did not recognize it immediately, the Lord was showing me the concrete reality of the community environment that supported the growth and development of our marriage and our conjugal spirituality.
>
> Re-entry into that Married Couple Group, though it felt awkward at times, made me aware of what I had been missing and helped me to see the truth of St. John Paul II's Rule. It was an experience of the importance of

---

[120] Part 1, chapter 3.

community to "supporting the dignity of the person in all we do" and for supporting marriage and married couples too.

## The Rule explains exactly how these communities ought to look.

When reviewing The Rule, we can see the important elements of a Christian community as St. John Paul II understood it. They would live out holy lives according to Christian moral norms and the Ten Commandments and seek ways to live out the spirit of the evangelical counsels. They would support each other in prayer, fellowship, and spiritual growth. They would continue to grow their education in the truth of marriage and family and pray for this truth to be known for their fellow group members, in the Church and in the world. More than merely this, the community must also reach outwards in love through an apostolate. This community is not random but intentional, by each member making a written promise of their commitment.[121] Fr. Kwiatkowski calls the *Humanae Vitae* groups designed by The Rule "a living community of spouses" that bears witness to the truth of marriage in love and states that these communities of spouses are, according to the words of Cardinal Wojtyła:

---

[121] *The Rule.*

... A certain equivalent of the diocesan seminary, an equivalent of a novitiate to the couples and families; an equivalent perhaps not yet entirely sufficient, but nevertheless real.[122]


## This community is a family of families.

St. John Paul II recognized that these communities will not be perfect, and just as in every large family, they will have challenges; however, they are necessary to live out faithful Christian lives in a time that demands a higher morality. These communities must continue to uphold the culture of the person. What he calls the "culture of the person" encompasses the dignity of the person (respect for each individual person no matter what) and the integral vision of the person (seeing each person "constantly in two moments: who he is and who he ought to be"[123] and, therefore, living in the tension of the messy middle between meeting people in the realness of life and yet calling them to holiness by showing them the great love God has created them for, [i.e., the Real and the Ideal]). The future of marriage depends on the support of each person in these Christian communities:

---

[122] Grygiel, 17, "secondo le parole del Cardinale Wojtyła: 'un certo equivalente del seminario diocesano, un equivalente del noviziato riguardo alle coppie e le famiglie; un equivalente magari ancora non del tutto sufficiente, ma tuttavia reale.'"
[123] *Reflections on Marriage, 2. Education for Marriage – the Culture of the Person.*

... The future of marriage, the future of all and each individual marriage, depends on each and every one of us, on the level of culture of the person in all of us.[124]

We felt this deep desire for community when we were first in Rome. And not just a desire but an affirmation that we *need* others' Christian friendship to grow in holiness. Praise God that we slowly found other married couples who were also studying theology, and we began to build strong friendships. It made a world of difference to be able to share our struggles with other faith-focused friends. Just hearing that we weren't alone, that others had similar struggles, lightened our spirits. We all shared the ridiculous antics in our lives and had good laughs. These same friends would also meet for Mass and celebrate feast days together. Through this small community of friends, we found our courage to continue on, and love broke in.

## Community is necessary for conjugal spirituality.

It is the community that helps support each married couple as they strive, with a reliance on grace, for Christian perfection and as they grow in their own

---

[124] *Reflections on Marriage, 2. Education for Marriage – the Culture of the Person.*

conjugal spirituality, which allows them to not only live a holy life but to live it with lasting joy.

# 11

## THE REAL AND THE IDEAL: *THE INTEGRAL VISION OF THE PERSON* THE RULE, #1

Having read part 1 and the introduction to the accompanying texts, you have seen this theme come around often. What St. John Paul II called the 'integral vision of the person' we have dubbed *The Real and the Ideal*. It is seeing the human person in all his entirety, and, therefore, not merely seeing him (or her) as they are now but also always keeping in mind who they are meant to be. When the first point explains that this Rule is from real experiences of married couples in Wojtyła's pastoral ministry, this emphasizes that we cannot take theology (the Ideal) apart from our experience (the Real). We must keep both pieces in mind at all times. We must see each person "constantly in two moments: *who he is* and *who he ought to be*."[125] We must stop and acknowledge the actual challenges

---

[125] *Reflections on Marriage, 2. Education for Marriage – the Culture of the Person.*

that others are experiencing (the Real). Yet, while we sympathize, listen, and care for spouses in their realness, we do not leave them there. We lovingly call each other to holiness (the Ideal).

This is important to us because we have had the experience of being invited into a group of faithful couples and their families and felt out of place. We showed up with great hopes to join a group of couples who wanted to really live their faith, but we were a little shocked when we got there. No one came up and welcomed us. Theresa felt uncomfortable because all the women had a particular way they dressed, and she stood out. No one attempted to comfort our uneasiness or "bring us in" to explain what was happening or how to join in. We got glances from people but no smiles. It seemed that we were not holy enough to be in their group. We remember thinking how gloomy everyone seemed, yet they held a certain air of self-assured sanctity. We tried to start conversations but were treated as outsiders. They seemed like nice people in general and probably didn't know how they were coming across to others, but we just started counting the minutes until we could gracefully exit. When we left, we had a discussion right then and there that if we ever had a group we were leading, everyone would be welcome. Joy would be the goal and being real would be as important as striving for holiness. Because, let's be honest, you will never become holy if you are not humble enough to recognize your realness.

### The human *person* is the subject through whose eyes we must try to see.

Personalism was important to St. John Paul II. 'Personalism' is a philosophical category in which one brings all objective truths to encounter the subject: the person. And if we can stretch our minds to try to see spouses through his eyes, through the lens of St. John Paul II's personalistic vision of man, we enter into the tension of the mystery of humanity. Our lives are not neat, tidy, easy things to explain. We are complicated and messy. For example, when theologians first argued over *Humanae Vitae*, there were many deeply intellectual arguments; however, it seems like it boiled down to two groups. On the one side, people looked at man *as he is*. They argued that it was too difficult, and life is too hard. On the other side, people looked at man *as he ought to be*. They argued this teaching was theologically true because of natural law and must be followed. Yet, this argument could come across as callous and ignores the struggles of real couples. St. John Paul II invites us to see each person in both instances: who they are and who they ought to be. Only when we get comfortable with the uncomfortable, and only when we sympathize and care for others in their current situations without judgment, and only when we aim our lives and encourage others to strive for holiness and Christian perfection can we build the culture of the person. Let's look a little deeper into St. John Paul II's personalist vision of humanity. Does this mean that we discount the truth? No. Only the truth will set us free. However, it means that we accept first the person, as they are, then call them to the truth.

## The Real and the Ideal takes us into the imperfect tension between our daily challenges and God's ideal for us.

St. John Paul II explains that being a person, man is always "spiritually individualized and free"[126] meaning he is one who has an intellect and free will. Man in his totality is an embodied spirit, and all that he does, he does *as a person*. This personalistic vision of man sees the human person as a whole: in his body and in his spirit, and in who he is and who he ought to be. He affirms this integral vision by explaining that his ideas stem from actual experiences of married couples (man as he is) and that one must "make theology encounter experience."[127] However, he does not remain only on the side of experience but balances this total vision by exhorting man to always strive for the ideal (man as he ought to be): "there is a recommendation, or even obligation, to pursue perfection." [128] A tension is created in this vision of man that juxtaposes the daily hardships and struggles of each particular human person with the ideal of what

---

[126] *Reflections on Marriage.*, 1. *At the Foundations of Personalism, a. The Order of Person.*
[127] *Love is the Moral Foundation of Marriage,* introductory paragraphs.
[128] *Ibid.*

God has called the human person to be in Christian perfection and holiness.

We can feel this tension when we are real with ourselves. Seeing our own faults takes humility and patience. Even St. Paul says, "I do not understand what I do. For what I want to do I do not do, but what I hate I do," (Rom 7:15). Do you ever have that feeling when you are humming along in your spiritual life and someone accuses you of something? Perhaps it was an unintentional slight or something you said, and your heart sinks to your stomach, and you feel a sort of panic set in. You realize it was your fault, but you never intended to hurt someone; yet, you did. It can burden us and depress us to feel our own weaknesses. Patience is required to live in this tension between the real and the ideal, as St. Padre Pio says:

> Those who aspire to a pure love of God actually need patience not so much with others but with themselves. To acquire perfection, you need to put up with your own imperfections. I tell you to tolerate them patiently, but that does not mean you should cherish them or be fond of them. Humility is nourished through this suffering ... our imperfections, my son, will be with us until we die; we cannot walk without touching the ground.[129]

---

[129] Gianluigi Pasquale, *Padre Pio's Spiritual Direction for Every Day*, (Franciscan Media: Cincinnati, 2011), 107.

Marriage cannot be only discussed
theoretically because it gets very real very
fast, especially considering the one-flesh
union of husband and wife.

Now let's bring this vision of the person into understanding what marriage is. When viewing marriage through this lens, one cannot overlook the *realness* of the fusion between flesh and spirit within the relationship of husband and wife. As St. John Paul II explained, it is precisely because the state of marriage involves a powerful action of the body in their sexual union, that one cannot merely theorize about marriage in only the spiritual sense. When a man loves a woman, it is an act of a person toward a person, and as such, it must be elevated to the dignity of the person (as understood in this integral vision). Not just their love ideologically but also every aspect of their marriage must be elevated to the dignity of the person. It would perhaps be simpler to view marriage only theoretically or only as it pertains directly to God. However, this is exactly the thinking that St. John Paul II says is not enough: "The idea [of marriage] needs to turn into reality."[130] As we seek to grow in our own marriages and encourage other couples, there is a constant balancing act of incorporating both pieces of the vision of the person: the real with the ideal.

Even as a priest, St. John Paul II was not afraid to look at real problems, which shows a genuine sensitivity to the concerns of women and men as they

---

[130] *Ibid., 4. Christian Perfection in Marriage.*

raise their families. When he mentions the particular stresses upon a mother and father, he comments that, "We also need to listen to their voices as they do not say it without reason."[131] However, neither is he afraid to call these couples to Christian perfection, for he says that marriage can maintain itself in an authentically Christian way "only on the condition of *striving towards perfection*."[132]

## Bishop Wojtyła addressed contraception within the dignity of the person seven years before *Humanae Vitae* was written.

He explains that we cannot accept the non-Catholic view of allowing all contraceptive options. It is not because we do not agree with the idea that a married couple ought to be free to discern their family size but because of the inherent morality that lies behind such thinking. Here he explains that it is not enough to merely assert natural law and demand married couples be faithful to nature. This would be only looking at the ideal without taking the real into account. Although the argument is correct, it falls on deaf ears for it fails to address the multifaceted situations in which couples find themselves. The people will hear it only as insensitive to the needs of real life.

---

[131] *Ibid.*, 6. *"Fidelity to Nature" or "Fidelity to Grace"?*
[132] *Ibid.*, 5. *Need to Get Out of the "Dead End."* Emphasis added.

Explaining again from experience, he notes that total fidelity to nature would produce large families and with the shifting socioeconomic culture, many parents find this a legitimate strain. Doing this "would mean a number of children often exceeding the strength of today's overworked mothers, and of fathers struggling to earn enough to meet the needs of the family—here, we also need to listen to their voices."[133] This fidelity to nature or looking only at the ideal, he says, is not enough for this new understanding of marriage in order to take into consideration the needs of the person.

It can be easy to apply our own experience to others. While this can help us sympathize with others, we have to resist the idea that what works best for us must be best for everyone. The challenge is to meet each couple within their own real and not gloss over it or offer blanket statements of "ought to" because we don't know their internal struggles. Listening to them is key.

## The grace of the sacrament of marriage gives us the strength to live God's way.

St. John Paul II does not reject the natural law arguments but says we must be sensitive to the real needs of the couples as well. Yet, he doesn't leave them in their difficulties. He says that when couples must practice periodic abstinence, they need faithfulness to

---

[133] *Ibid., 6. "Fidelity to Nature" or "Fidelity to Grace"?*

grace more than faithfulness simply to nature. He is still calling them to the ideal but doing so in a way that incorporates and is sensitive to their real-life struggles. St. John Paul II emphasizes that this is where the tension lies. The Church is right in speaking of fidelity to nature, but when a couple is faced with practicing periodic abstinence, this is not enough. Such a teaching is difficult to accept and live out in man's fallen nature; they need fidelity to grace. This is how he balances the real and the ideal — through the grace found in the sacrament of marriage.

He also explains that a simple ban against contraception, without an explanation as to why, only incites misunderstandings and opposition. Again, it is disregarding their experiences as persons. And yet, he always points them to holiness and Christian perfection. He says, "It seems that conjugal abstinence (even if only temporary) is difficult to practice if it isn't supported by certain, even modest, pursuit of perfection available in marriage."[134] In other words, a couple will not be able to joyfully live out authentic Christian marriage without striving for holiness and Christian perfection as a couple (i.e., conjugal spirituality).

We heard a homily recently that puts this in a different perspective, giving us a sort of paradigm shift toward it. The priest asked if we follow God's ways out of obligation or out of love. We can follow the teaching of the Church because we 'have to,' or we can follow it because we love God and want to grow closer to Him.

---

[134] *Ibid.*

When a couple does discern that they need to postpone conceiving a child and must take up the cross of abstaining at certain times, do they do this out of obligation? This would seem to align with what St. John Paul II called the fidelity to nature. Or do they rejoice having another cross to lovingly offer to God? This is definitely a challenge! Rejoicing at any cross is a challenge. Yet, this is the fidelity to grace and the striving for holiness that would make rejoicing at a cross possible. This is not to say we seek out crosses, but that when one comes along, as always does in life, we take the opportunity to offer it to God in love.

Jesus told us there would be crosses and even said, "If anyone would come after me, let him deny himself and take up his cross and follow me" (Mt 16:24). Yet, by our own human efforts, this is impossible. This is where grace is necessary. God gives us his own life to help us love as He loves! Let us listen to St. Paul here: "But he said to me, 'My grace is sufficient for you, for my power is made perfect in weakness.' Therefore I will boast all the more gladly of my weaknesses, so that the power of Christ may rest upon me." (2Cor 12:9).

## When couples see the beautiful closeness to God possible in marriage, the burdens will be easier to bear.

This need for the balance between the real and the ideal is clear when St. John Paul II titles one of his sections *In Line with Reality*. He says we must get to the truth about marriage and bring theories into the real lives of ordinary spouses. We must change our lens of how we view marriage. If our view remains at a basic level and we do not give the spouses much to aim for, the burdens we are asking of them will be too great indeed. Instead, "presume more to be able to demand more (just as much as we need)."[135] When couples have a reason to reach for holiness, the burdens will be more easily borne. We must consistently acknowledge and affirm the real everyday life struggles while at the same time point couples to holiness. This striving for holiness is how the realness of life is lived in joy.

Steve and Allison, a couple in a WCI Married Couple Group, share:

> Reflecting on the real (who man is) and the ideal (who man ought to be) from The Rule, we can't help but think about how God's plan for our family is completely different from our plan. Our plan (the ideal) was to have children as soon as possible and as many as possible. We wanted to fill our home and share our blessings with them. God's plan (the real) has been anything but that. While we were blessed to conceive one child (the ideal), we lost our little John Cecilia after eleven weeks (the real).
>
> Since then, we've been unable to conceive or successfully adopt a child. And even though this reality was never part of our plan, we've

---

[135] *Ibid., 8. In Line with Reality.*

been blessed with the grace of accepting God's plan for us. We've discovered a spiritual parenthood that has been, in many ways, very rewarding. The following quotes from St. Josemaría Escrivá have brought us much comfort as we continue on this journey:

"Often God does not give children because He is asking them for something more … There is, then, no reason for feeling they are failures … If the married couple has interior life, they will understand that God is urging them to make their lives a generous Christian service, a different apostolate from the one they would have fulfilled with their children, but an equally marvelous one …

God, who always rewards, will fill with a deep joy those souls who have had the generous humility of not thinking of themselves."

"God in his providence has two ways of blessing marriages: one, by giving them children; and the other, sometimes, because he loves them so much, by not giving them children. I don't know which is the better blessing."[136]

---

[136]Josemaría Escrivá as cited on https://www.escrivaworks.org/book/-conversations-point-96.htm and https://catholiccurrent.org/wp-content/uploads/2018/09/TWIM-4-50-Podcast-Reflection.pdf.

The integral vision of the person is this balance between being present to our family's daily needs — even through challenges — and always reaching for God.

This can seem like an uncomfortable idea. How can husband and wife live peacefully in this tension between the real and the ideal? It is easier to go to the extreme. Yet, it is more difficult to be open to God in those extremes. The over-spiritualized life that doesn't admit the struggles does not allow God to help them in those struggles. They cannot move forward spiritually if they do not see where they are in the present. Nor can the couple who give up on pursuing the ideal make spiritual strides because they believe it to be impossible. It is in the messy middle where we feel vulnerable and shaky and where we see our faults but we never stop pleading for God's merciful love that God can work in amazing ways. Spouses can draw strength from Jesus Christ. This is where power is found because His becoming flesh "did not take place as a form of accusation of humanity but rather its justification, or as a way to pull it out of the original devaluation and weakness that humans defer to so

---

*Editor's note*: Since writing this reflection, this couple has welcomed home a beautiful, adopted, baby daughter, born on the Feast of Our Lady of Fatima. What amazing things God can do in our lives when we surrender all to Him!

often."[137] In Christ, we see the body redeemed and made holy.

St. John Paul II says it is the responsibility of the Christian community to uphold this culture of the person, and when the culture of the person begins to fall in modern society, we must intentionally create communities that uphold it.

---

[137] *Reflections on Marriage, 3. Economy and Personalism.*

# 12

## *HUMANAE VITAE*[138]
## THE RULE, #1

Cardinal Wojtyła created The Rule to, as he says, actualize *Humanae Vitae* within the daily lives of married couples. In other words, The Rule is meant to help spouses live *Humanae Vitae* — to infuse their marriages and family lives with its truth, allow divine Love to enter in, and find lasting joy. He even sees *Humanae Vitae* as so important and central to The Rule that he suggests the groups could call themselves '*Humanae Vitae* Groups.'

There is so much that has been said on the truth of *Humanae Vitae*.[139] For our purposes, we will focus on

---

[138] For a gripping read, we recommend Mary Eberstadt, *Adam and Eve after the Pill*, (Ignatius Press: San Francisco, 2012). Also, to understand HUMANAE VITAE and the logic of its truth, see Janet Smith, *Why Humanae Vitae was Right: a Reader*, (Ignatius Press: San Francisco, 1993).

[139] See the appendix for extra resources and more suggestions on books about *Humanae Vitae*.

St. John Paul II's view of the document at that time and the integral vision of the person found within *Humanae Vitae* that affirms his view. We will proceed by limiting our focus to looking at *Humanae Vitae* as Cardinal Wojtyła addressed it.

We know from part 1 that *Humanae Vitae* was not well-received. It took great courage, Fr. Kwiatkowski[140] notes, that Cardinal Wojtyła didn't merely write a few articles in support of *Humanae Vitae* but created The Rule to help implement the teaching into his diocese. The premise and existence of The Rule itself is a positive endorsement to *Humanae Vitae*.[141]

## St. John Paul II shows us that St. Paul VI wrote *Humanae Vitae* with a view of the integral vision of the person.

As we noted in the previous chapter, St. John Paul II explains that understanding and supporting marriage requires the integral vision of the person. He tells us that the teaching of *Humanae Vitae* must also be read with this view in mind. Remember, this integral vision of the person includes always approaching the human person with two moments in mind: who man is and who he ought to be, the real and the ideal. Yet, we are not just placing this view onto *Humanae Vitae*. A careful reading of the document will show it was

---

[140] Fr. Kwiatkowski was the priest who revived these texts and translated them to Italian.
[141] Grygiel, 16.

written with this scope in mind. For example, St. Paul VI stated in the document itself:

It is the whole man and the whole mission to which he is called that must be considered: both its natural, earthly aspects and its supernatural, eternal aspects.[142]

Although he had to speak to a particular question and put forth answers to objective moral norms, St. Paul VI keeps this within the personalistic perspective and therefore subjective. Not subjective in the sense that everything is relative but in the sense that we must look at the subject, the person, to whom these moral norms apply. In other words, he places the objective discussion of this particular problem within the integral vision of the person. Here's another example:

*[Marriage] is in reality the wise and provident institution of God the Creator, whose purpose was to effect in man His loving design.* As a consequence, husband and wife, through that mutual gift of themselves, which is specific and exclusive to them alone, develop that union of two persons in which they perfect one another, cooperating with God in the generation and rearing of new lives.[143]

St. Paul VI affirms the integral vision of the person because he is seeing man in not only his present

---

[142] *Humanae Vitae*, 7.
[143] *Ibid.*, 8.

circumstances, "which is specific and exclusive to them alone," but also in who he was meant to be. "*[Marriage] is in reality the wise and provident institution of God."*

# The key point of *Humanae Vitae* is that God, and not man, is the author of marriage and human sexuality.

Fr. Vincent Twomey, SVD, a priest and moral theologian who wrote extensively on the impact of *Humanae Vitae* on moral theology, explains the modern culture's different view of man. He says that in this industrialized culture, man's self-understanding is as a maker or producer of things, and the body is seen simply as "raw material to be shaped and used at will."[144] At the heart of the teaching of *Humanae Vitae*, then, is the truth that God, and not man, is the author of marriage and human sexuality.

Paula and Jimmy, a couple in a WCI Married Couple Group, share:

> We started out our marriage without the help of a clear understanding of Catholic teaching. We were a contracepting couple experiencing the effects of living without the full flow of God's grace in our marriage and in our lives. In time, we came to the use of NFP because of health problems caused by artificial birth

---

[144] D. Vincent Twomey, *Moral Theology after Humanae Vitae*, (Four Courts Press Ltd: Dublin, 2010), 197.

control. But the blessings we received from conforming our marriage to God's plan and Catholic teaching were far more than just a lack of illness. Yes, the infections were gone, but we both agree that the beauty of our conjugal life became dynamic, like moving from black and white to color, or 2D to 3D, or from mono to stereo. There were elements of unknown potential that entered our union and created an excitement we had been denying ourselves. And God's grace flooded our family! I know we have a wealth of blessings that could not be possible without our openness to His plan for our marriage as expressed by *Humanae Vitae*.

Even now, as the season of fertility in our marriage has passed, God still blesses our union. Recognizing early on that both unitive and procreative aspects of our conjugal life need to be honored, not only have I felt my husband's respect for the intricate way God has created my feminine body, but I have come to understand the deep need my husband has for the closeness we experience in the unitive embrace. Unitive and procreative — both need to be kept intact — God decides the outcome. We're still open to God's will in our lives!

God calls us to a love that is a truly and integrally honest love.

St. Paul VI reminds us that everything must be seen in light of man's final destiny and that love must be human, total, faithful, and fruitful.[145] He also affirms each act "must remain open to the transmission of life."[146] In following Vatican II, which claimed the criteria for discerning judgements about the transmission of life must be *objective*, Paul VI proclaims that "it is not licit, even for the gravest reasons, to do evil so that good might follow."[147] In the rejection of contraception, he promotes the practices of NFP that work with the woman's natural fertility cycle and build self-mastery. Being open to life in this way is "a truly and integrally honest love."[148]

Aaron, a husband in a WCI Married Couple Group, shares:

> Understanding the history behind *Humanae Vitae* was important for my wife and I to know. It gave us a perspective of what the Church was thinking during the time of increasing acceptance of the use of contraception and ultimately abortion.
>
> Knowing this information allows us to pray more intentionally for the world that they see how beautiful it is to give and receive your spouse as a sincere gift.

---

[145] *HV*, 9.
[146] *Ibid.*, 11.
[147] *Ibid.*, 14.
[148] *Ibid.*, 16.

Another key point is freedom in the context of mastery of self.

My wife and I had conversations about what this means for us in our marriage as we discern God's will with how big of a family He wants to give us. We sometimes think that this conversation is just between a husband and a wife, but it also involves God, as He is the author of life.

God has reminded us of this time and again with not one ... not two ... but three "surprise" pregnancies. What we thought we could control, even in a moral sense through the licit use of natural family planning, is actually something God wants full control of in our marriage.

My wife often refers to NFP as "PFP" — Providential Family Planning. Even if a couple chooses to use NFP in their marriage, God can still do what He wills in their union because of that openness to each other and His acting grace upon them. Studying *Humanae Vitae* through our Married Couple Group has only solidified our conviction that this is the only way to live out our marriage. Even when it may throw us a few surprises, God's plans are always better than ours.

We, as human *persons*, and made in the image
and likeness of God, are made to be *in relation*
with another.

   Cardinal Wojtyła wrote articles in support of
*Humanae Vitae* in 1969 and pointing out its
anthropological vision.[149] He explains that a further
understanding of the meaning of the person is one who
is *in relation*,[150] and this is a reflection of the
personhood of the Trinitarian nature of God. Each
Person of the Trinity is understood as being in relation
to another. We say "God the Father," but what is *father*
except one who has a child? How do we understand

---

[149] It is important to note that there is a complex history behind
*Humanae Vitae*, especially including St. John Paul II and an
integral vision of the person.  Before writing *Humanae Vitae*,
Cardinal Wojtyła was one of the theologians invited to be on the
commission that considered the issue.  He was unable to attend
the commission in person because the Polish government
refused to issue him a passport; however, he organized a
commission in Krakow to investigate the issue.  The results of
this investigation were organized into a memorandum and
offered a much more compelling and personalistic explanation
than we read in *Humanae Vitae*.  "The controversy was
inevitable, but it might not have been so debilitating had the
Pope taken Cardinal Wojtyła's counsel more thoroughly,"
(Weigel, 208).  "Had the Kraków commission's memorandum
shaped the argumentation of *Humanae Vitae* more decisively, a
more intelligent and sensitive debate might have ensued." (*Ibid.*,
210).  So, while *Humanae Vitae* does contain this integral vision of
the person, it is important to understand that it was not enough.
St. John Paul II knew that there was more to say on the subject
and spent his papacy fulfilling this.
[150] Cardinal Karol Wojtyła, "The Anthropological Vision of
*Humanae Vitae*," January 16 (L'Osservatore Romano: Rome,
1969), 3.

"God the Son" except by one who has a parent? Each Divine Person is understood by this 'in relation' character. So, too, we as human persons, who are made in the image and likeness of God, are made to be *in relation* with another.

When one gives a gift of oneself to another, they fulfill their own personhood and become more clearly the image and likeness of God. In marriage, this total gift of self to another must include their fertility. To separate the unitive and procreative dimensions of the marital act, Wojtyła explained, is to divide the unity of a person, which is contrary to Christian view. This division is Cartesian[151] and enforces the idea that only the mind matters (and the body does not) and is utilitarian, which says that the body can be used but does not really matter. It is from this article that we have previously quoted Wojtyła's wise words explaining that *Humanae Vitae* gives us the conditions that will safeguard self-giving, authentic love and will preserve the ontology (or essence) of authentic spousal love from falsification.[152]

Arguably the most controversial Church document in the last century, *Humanae Vitae* has been the topic of much theological disputation. The "controversial" label came not because it departed from Ecclesial tradition but because of the backlash it received when

---

[151] Editor's note: This adjective means 'of or relating to René Descartes or his philosophy.' René Descartes said, "I think, therefore I am." This rejection of the material world and centrality of importance on the mind created a dualism in which only the mind and not the body had any essential meaning.

[152] Milne, 65.

it was promulgated. In proclaiming within *Humanae Vitae* that "each and every marriage act must remain open to the transmission of life,"[153] St. Paul VI was affirming teaching that was well established within the Church dating back to the first century. [154]

When we were in Rome as newlyweds and starving graduate students, we needed to use NFP to postpone pregnancy. It was a bit of a dying to self. Theresa had irregular cycles, and although NFP did work, it took a lot of caution. We found ourselves frustrated. We were still trying to fit worldly ideals into this living God's way. The world puts sexuality as the high point of life; they'd say if you aren't free to have sex, you aren't free at all.

Following God's way, we place the priority on love more than just sex. Can I really love my spouse if I am not respecting all of him or her, including their fertility? That doesn't mean that it isn't still challenging to abstain when we need to. Our desire for sexual intimacy is a gift from God. But when we surrender even this to God, He can bring our love into a whole new realm, a place found deeper within the heart of our heavenly Father.

Throughout our marriage, keeping love primary, it also opened a deeper level of communication and fostered a sweetness of affection between us, which were vital to us being able to get through some

---

[153] *HV*, 11.
[154] See appendix for just a few of the many examples to support this.

challenging times (even the loss of a child). We realized that *Humanae Vitae* is about allowing God to be fully in charge of our love. And we have no regrets. That is why we are so grateful to be in a Married Couple Group that understands the struggles and strives to live out the truths of *Humanae Vitae* with joy. We have never felt so supported in our striving to live out the truth!

## *Humanae Vitae* is the heart of the teaching of marriage and family.

It was because of the great opposition to *Humanae Vitae* that many rose to explain and defend it throughout the decades that followed. The Church is indebted to the theologians, priests, and bishops who analyzed, clarified, and even expounded upon the teaching of *Humanae Vitae,* answering the call of St. Paul VI as well as St. John Paul II, when he was pope, who invited theologians:

> To unite their efforts in order to collaborate with the hierarchical magisterium and to commit themselves to the task of illustrating ever more clearly the biblical foundations, the ethical grounds, and the personalistic reasons behind this doctrine [on the proper regulation of family size].[155]

St. John Paul II, during his papacy, expanded and advanced God's plan for human sexuality more than

---

[155] John Paul II, *Familiaris Consortio*, 31.

any other. Although *Humanae Vitae* was written with
an integral vision of the person, it did not go far
enough in explaining the beauty of God's plan human
love.[156] St. John Paul II showed great respect for
conjugal love when he explained that the "'one flesh'
union between man and woman is the sacramental
reflection of God, which renders the mystery of the
Trinity truly present."[157] Through his multitude of
teachings, especially *Familiaris Consortio, Mulieris
Dignitatem,* and the treatises of the *Theology of the Body,*
many more clergy, theologians, and lay faithful have
further understood the teaching of *Humanae Vitae.*

---

[156] *Cf.* Weigel, 210.
[157] *Mulieris Dignitatem,* 7.

# 13

## CHRISTIAN MORALITY: *ENCOUNTER WITH CHRIST*[158] THE RULE, #3

St. John Paul II includes living according to the norms of Christian morality in the third point of The Rule. He mentions the Commandments and principles of Christian morality, but also finding a way to embrace the spirit of the evangelical counsels within their married and family life (poverty, obedience, and chastity). The vows of the evangelical counsels should not be taken in the strict sense like a consecrated religious would follow them; however, there would be ways that a couple could embrace the spirit of the counsels.

---

[158] We wish to emphasize that these chapters are not an exhaustive explanation of each topic but an explanation of the themes as they are intended in The Rule by examining them in the contemporary texts of Wojtyła.

## Embracing the *spirit* of the vow of poverty: the relationship we have with material things.

What may it look like to embrace the spirit of the counsels in married and family life? St. John Paul II gives us some examples to consider. Pondering the spirit of the vow of poverty, this could mean a certain detachment from the material things that the couple owns and a renunciation of excessive indulgence. In fact, he says, as we work to build community to change culture, it is a requirement:

> Christianity is still convinced that living in a community requires, above all, high moral standards in which the spiritual ideal enables renunciation from some material goods — or from a certain relationship with these goods.[159]

Embracing the spirit of the vow of poverty concerns the relationship we have with the material things we own. For personal reflection, we could ask ourselves how upset we would get when someone accidentally breaks, perhaps, the china plate handed down from our great-great-grandmother? What would our reaction be to driving up to seeing our home on fire? Our reaction ought to point to how attached or detached we are to the material goods. The goal, in this case, as St. John Paul II explained in The Rule, would be to "constantly rework" how the spirit of poverty is lived in our family. We must take stock of how well we are remaining detached from the gifts that God has

---

[159] *Reflections on Marriage, 3. Economy and Personalism.*

provided in our life. Material things are not bad in themselves, but it is our relationship with these items that is the focus of concern.

Once on her return from studies in England, Theresa had brought home a lovely souvenir mug bought in London and beautifully painted. On the second day she was home, the little ones were playing downstairs. From our bedroom, she heard a commotion and a crash, which was followed by silence. She came down to find her only souvenir from the trip broken in pieces on the floor. Yes, she cried. Being exhausted and pregnant may have had something to do with it. But it seemed like the final straw in a series of things, and she just pouted. Why, she thought, couldn't she have nice things? And looking at the three munchkins in time-out, all sorrowful with sad, puppy-dog eyes of remorse, she remembered that it was, indeed, just a mug. She forgave them, and they scampered off presumably to start mischief somewhere else. Enjoying the material gifts God has given us is not wrong; He wants us to live in joy. It's when we give more meaning to things than they ought to have that things begin to go awry. Sweet puppy-dog eyes of toddlers are often good reminders to reset priorities.

# Embracing the *spirit* of obedience: the virtue of humility.

There is no more effective means to holiness than the virtue of humility. Yet, what might this look like? Choosing to respect the decision of a pastor, for example, even if you might disagree with him, could be an example of this. When our pride begins to damage our relationships with others, we can see how much that robs our joy. True humility is when we forget ourselves so that we can love God and love others. When we allow God to be the final judge and when we let go in these situations, amazing grace comes into our lives.

Living out the faith in a culture that has abandoned moral norms is in itself an act of obedience. We can further live out this vow of obedience not merely by following the Christian precepts but by learning more about them. Then, they are not simply a burden to bear; instead, through a deeper understanding and with the help of grace, they bring us joy.

## Embracing the *spirit* of chastity: found beautifully within conjugal spirituality.

Even within his treatise on the Theology of the Body, St. John Paul II says that chastity is "at the center of conjugal spirituality."[160] Chastity gives couples a desire to respect the dignity of the marital act. Yet, chastity displays itself not merely within the sexual act, but throughout the lives of the spouses. This is their

---

[160] St. John Paul II, *Man and Woman He Created Them*, (Pauline Books and Media: Boston, 2006) 131:2.

conjugal spirituality—the life of grace pouring into every aspect of their united life.[161] A true communion of persons is only reached when husband and wife are united not only through the body but also in their hearts and minds. When we allow God's grace to fill up our nature, we can be attentive to the whole person and a true unity can be formed.[162]

St. John Paul II taught us that the special grace available to us in marriage is truly real. And more than that, it is always available to us.[163] Spouses can tap into it at any moment of their day and use it to cultivate the virtue of chastity, which nourishes conjugal spirituality and helps it to grow.

St. John Paul II leaves it to each individual married couple to allow the Holy Spirit to guide them on how this will look within their own marriage, encouraging each couple to "rework" it often.

Jimmy and Paula share their experience of how their ideal was confronted with a real and most difficult situation and God's grace sustained them:

> In our ongoing conversion as a married couple, striving to live the norms of Christian morality, the ideal frequently is confronted by the real. One such powerful example of this in our lives also encountered the spirit of poverty,

---

[161] *Ibid., Cf.* 132:4.
[162] *Ibid., Cf.* 109:4.
[163] *Love is the Moral Foundation of Marriage,* 7. *The Sacramental Grace is Not Just a Theory.*

obedience, and chastity through the grace of our life in Christ. When fertility returned after our third child, we had "the talk."

Being older parents and a homeschooling family with only one income, there could have been legitimate reasons to postpone conception through NFP, but Jimmy responded with, "I trust God. He won't give us children that He won't provide for." These words were prophetic in many ways.

We conceived our next child, and all seemed well until the eighteenth week when tests and ultrasounds revealed that our baby, Patrick, had trisomy 18, a genetic condition that causes 70 percent of these babies to die in utero.

Even if he lived, our baby was expected to have severe birth defects. We were asked multiple times, "Do you know what you want to do?" and "Do you want to terminate the pregnancy?" But we responded that we would trust God with his life.

Our one prayer was that we would see our baby with his eyes open, even if just for a few hours. God granted our prayers. We had six blessed weeks with Patrick as well as everything we could have needed:

prayers, emotional support, medical help, medical bills paid, diapers, cards, gifts, childcare... Through God's grace, He turned our spirit of obedience, chastity, and poverty into profound blessings.

## Our faith is an encounter with Jesus Christ.

In both of the accompanying texts, St, John Paul II emphasizes that authentic Christianity is more than following a daily checklist of good deeds. It is a loving relationship with Jesus Christ to whom we strive to orient our lives. He is the source and embodiment of our faith.[164] He calls everyone to holiness and to communion with Him.

We orient our lives towards Christ by following His commands out of love for God. This is done in embracing the Person of Christ as we walk the path of faith. Do you remember when we discussed how to reach goals in the first chapter? We said there is nothing you can *do* to make God love you. God loves you right now with infinite abundance! Even if you never did any of the things on your holiness checklist, God loves you. He doesn't just tolerate you until you get your life in order. He loves you with a passionate, vibrant love, even when you sin. His love is not conditional. He loves you because of *who He is*, not because of what you've done. You don't need to be perfect before you approach God; God wants to meet

---

[164] *Cf.* Saward, 94.

you right where you are. He wants to come into your life and fill it with His divine, merciful love.

Our goal—life with God—is at our doorstep; it is not far off but right before you. He will help you on your spiritual journey, imbuing each of those holy actions with more of His grace. Instead of it being a list of tasks to achieve then reaching the goal at the end, our Goal is already with us. We must walk in the path of His love and do the actions that help us open our hearts more and more to His grace and merciful love.

Your holiness is not found in merely doing the actions but in the way you allow God to meet you in those actions, in the way you allow each moment of grace to affect your heart. We continue to do what is right while realizing that we already have a relationship with a loving God. The Rule points the way to open ourselves, and our marriages, to be more receptive to God's merciful love. It guides us in love, and we find ourselves nestled in the heart of the Father.

# 14

## MARRIAGE UNITY AND CONJUGAL SPIRITUALITY THE RULE, #2, #4

In the second point of The Rule, St. John Paul II insists that both spouses must participate in the Married Couple Group and that one spouse cannot join without the other. This is because the main purpose of the Married Couple Groups is to build the couple's conjugal spirituality. This may seem unfair. If a husband or wife want to learn about marriage, but their spouse is not interested, should they be penalized for this? St. John Paul II is not discriminating anyone here; rather, he is calling the couple to a higher level of spiritual holiness. There is a uniqueness to the Married Couple Groups that The Rule creates, which puts them in their own category. Of course, individuals are always encouraged to learn more about their faith, about how to live their marriage well, and how to strive to apply that. Every baptized person has his or her own relationship with God, and through the sacraments, St. John Paul II says, a person enters an "orbit of grace" with God. However, although education is a piece of the groups, the "main purpose" of The Rule is to cultivate conjugal spirituality, which can only be done when both spouses are involved.

Both spouses need to participate because conjugal spirituality is the special relationship God has with the husband and wife united together, which is made possible through the Sacrament of Marriage. These groups are a way to take married couples from good to great. They are Married Couple Groups, not women's groups or men's groups, and as such, these groups have a specific focus that requires both spouses' participation. One reason a spouse may not want to participate in this faith walk, St. John Paul II explains, is that they haven't been given much of a vision of marriage. He says this is why there is a "need for a re-education"[165] of the idea of marriage, which he has also explained as a needed "new model of marriage."[166] When couples have a vision of marriage as a vocation to seek spiritual holiness and not merely a 'natural relationship,' they will be more inclined to seek this goal together.

Allison and Steve, a couple from a WCI Married Couple Group, share their experience of the importance of marriage unity:

> When we were in the process of ordering our wedding rings, we had the words *Totus Tuus* (totally yours) engraved on the

---

[165] *Reflections on Marriage, 3. Economy and Personalism.*
[166] *Love is the Moral Foundation of Marriage, introductory paragraphs.*

inside of the bands. This was St. John Paul II's motto, which he also had engraved on his coat of arms as pope. We didn't quite know it at the time, but this desire to give ourselves totally to each other and to Jesus through Mary is what St. John Paul II calls marriage unity.

As The Rule teaches, marriage unity is about both of us promising to be fully involved. For us, it fully reflects the motto for our marriage to be free, total, faithful and fruitful. Since our wedding day, we have strived daily to freely give ourselves to the other person, to totally share everything (even our deepest secrets) with the other person, to be faithful to each other by putting their needs first, and to share our fruitful blessings with others. *Totus Tuus!*

## Conjugal Spirituality

Now we come to what is truly the heart of The Rule. The Rule states that developing conjugal spirituality is the main purpose of the Married Couple Groups. The reason this is because the couple's holiness hinges upon their conjugal spirituality. The Rule affirms *Humanae Vitae* not merely in an abstract way but in helping the teaching be actualized "in a concrete way within human life."[167] This actualization of *Humanae Vitae* within their life only happens through conjugal spirituality. Conjugal spirituality connects the grace of God to our everyday lives. We don't just understand the meaning of the teaching of *Humanae Vitae* but live it daily whether we are cleaning the dishes, or caring for our spouse, or enjoying a meal together. Christ's love works through our love, purifying it.

> This spirituality occurs precisely *within the sacramental nature* of their marriage and not without.[168]

This spirituality of the couple (their growth in holiness) occurs precisely within the sacramental nature of their marriage and not without.[169] This sacramental nature allows their marriage to reflect the spousal relationship between Christ and His bride, the Church. Again, the spiritual life of the couple is not merely a following of a set of rules, but:

> It is, in the first place, a concrete way in which the redeeming-spousal mystery is lived in the proper dimensions of conjugal and family life, which leads to sanctification.[170]

---

[167] Grygiel, 17, "in una forma concreta di vita umana."
[168] *Ibid.*
[169] *Ibid.*
[170] *Ibid.*

Conjugal spirituality not only plays a significant role in the accomplishment of the truth of *Humanae Vitae* in the life of the spouses; it makes living out such a personalistic vision of marriage possible.

Emily, a wife in a WCI Married Couple Group, shares:

> Since learning about conjugal spirituality through The Rule, God has invited us to more deeply experience this in our marriage. On one occasion, Aaron went on a trip out of state for his graduate studies for about a week while I stayed home with our children. Knowing Aaron's studies at his residency would be rigorous, with his passing the course contingent on his success there, I asked God to allow me to support Aaron at home through my prayers.
>
> On the final full day of his residency, Aaron gave a presentation that would account for a major part of his grade. That morning, I woke up with a fever. Being a nursing mother, I soon realized that I had developed a breast infection, seemingly out of nowhere. As the day went on, the fever and accompanying symptoms worsened.
>
> While praying through the suffering, I realized that God was allowing this suffering for Aaron's sake. The second day

of the fever was much the same, so I made plans to see a doctor the following morning. However, that evening, Aaron returned home safely from his trip.

Upon his return, the fever and infection left me. I truly sensed that my suffering was being allowed as an offering for my husband, and that God united us mystically even as we were physically apart. This was the first time we truly felt like we experienced conjugal spirituality in a tangible way in our marriage.

## What is conjugal spirituality?

In short, conjugal spirituality is the relationship between the Blessed Trinity and the couple, united as one and made possible through grace. Conjugal spirituality unites husband and wife so profoundly that they have one interior life. This sincere, spiritual unity "allows (one) to configure the conjugal and family life in a Christian way."[171] The married couple must be committed to seeking and forming this conjugal spirituality so that "the integral teachings of Jesus Christ on marriage and family, proclaimed by the Church, could be accomplished in their married life with full understanding and full love."[172] *It is conjugal*

---

[171] *The Rule, point 4.*
[172] *Ibid.*

*spirituality that actuates the truth of marriage within the concrete reality of daily, married life.*

## How is conjugal spirituality possible?

Let's look a little closer at this relationship between the union of spouses and the Blessed Trinity. It is made possible through the sacrament of marriage, and in order to understand this we need to first hear how St. John Paul II explains sacraments in general.

He says that sanctifying grace is offered to each person through every sacrament. When a baptized person receives grace, they have the potential to live a new spiritual life; in fact, it is a:

> ... Life that is supernatural; supernatural to what degree depends on this person's actualization of the resources of grace in his or her life.[173]

A person's degree of holiness correlates directly to his openness to grace in his life.

Each sacrament is efficacious, which means it brings about the reality it signifies: the sacrament:

> ... as a powerful sign of grace, creates in nature the forces that are supernatural, forces that allow for a full life of a human being—that is to say, life

[173] *Reflections on Marriage, 1. At the Foundations of Personalism, b. The Order of Grace.*

according to the plans and intentions of the Creator towards the mankind.[174]

However, there is a distinction between making the fullness of life possible and bringing it to fruition or completion. Grace is available and it is possible for man to live an extraordinary life in God, but man has a responsibility here. It doesn't happen automatically. It is left to man to open himself to grace and receive from the supernatural gifts the new spiritual life, and "enter in the orbit of grace."[175]

The sacrament of marriage is unique for two reasons. First, it is the only sacrament in which two people take part in one sacrament. Through the sacrament, "there are simultaneously two persons that enter the orbit of grace."[176] While each sacrament brings the recipient closer in his relationship with God, marriage in its uniqueness builds the relationship between God and the two spouses united as one. Two people walk into this communion, and in their union have a relationship with God. This is conjugal spirituality.

As St. John Paul II explains it, this unity is entered into freely by the two individuals, husband and wife. He is not saying this replaces one's individual relationship with God, which he affirms in his explanation of sacraments in general. Yet, this secondary relationship to God through their spiritual

---

[174] *Ibid.*, 1. *At the Foundations of Personalism, c. The Order of Sacrament.*
[175] *Ibid.*
[176] *Ibid.*

unity is what allows marriages to grow and thrive, actuating the truth in their daily life. Building conjugal spirituality brings the couple from good to great in their pursuit of joyful holiness.

Secondly, the sacrament of marriage is the only sacrament in which the faithful are the ministers. The husband and wife, by their vows, confer the sacrament on each other. Here is a startling insight from St. John Paul II: being the minister of the sacrament to one's spouse does not end at the altar on the wedding day. The spouses:

> ... Are for each other direct instruments of the action of God, they are like conductors to the current of life that is in God and of which they become partakers through the sacrament.[177]

Husband and wife, through the gift of supernatural grace, are the action of God in their spouse's life and together are caught up in the orbit of grace as their life is renewed into a supernatural life through "the mystery of grace that penetrates into nature."[178]

It is this sanctifying grace that offers the possibility of conjugal spirituality and holiness for couples, but it is left to the husband and wife to be open to and take advantage of these supernatural gifts.

We do need to be open to God's grace for Him to work. For example, being the "action of God" in your spouse's life is such a beautiful idea, but it is really true.

---

[177] *Ibid.*
[178] *Ibid.*, 1. At the Foundations of Personalism, b. The Order of Grace.

We have both experienced healing through our marriage. When Theresa was younger, she had a bout with anorexia in junior high, which was more an effect than a cause in itself. And even though the action of avoiding food stopped, the reasons she fell into that in the first place still hovered in her mind—like a darkness of unworthiness. From then until her college years, she had mentally separated herself from others, showing only her best side and thinking, if they really knew her, they wouldn't love her.

This was not their fault, but her own. She did not even give others a chance to love her because she still had this hovering cloud of self-loathing within her. When Theresa and Peter were engaged and through the first year of their marriage, they shared everything. Neither one of them held anything back, and she was so surprised that he didn't run screaming for the door. He still loved her! Even knowing all her faults, Peter loved her. Through his love, she was able to accept herself, accept God's love in a deeper way, and even begin to open herself up to others. Peter's unconditional, self-giving love allowed for her healing. God was truly working through Peter's love, and sacramental grace was present in his love, guiding her to accept our Father's love more fully and become more of the woman God created Theresa to be.

Conjugal spirituality creates a profound spiritual unity between the spouses.

Husband and wife, united in marriage, can deepen their union by cultivating their conjugal spirituality, in which "the journey of a couple is *one* journey made by two."[179] What a stark contrast this is to a more secular idea of marriage, where spouses may feel as though they are sexually compatible persons who share life and schedules as long as it continues to be convenient and enjoyable. Remember that for Christian spouses, their holiness "is not found outside, but within their sacramental communion that embodies the spousal love of Christ and of the Church."[180] The closer they become to one another and to God, the more perfectly they will embody and reflect that love of Christ for His Church.

Through conjugal spirituality, their personalities are not lost but perfected.

St. John Paul II even says this profound unity might make someone fearful.[181] Can you hear the questions? Does that mean I have to have the same style of prayer as my spouse? Does "profound unity" mean we have to be the exact same? What if I appreciate Benedictine spirituality and my spouse prefers Dominican—will this affect our conjugal spirituality? I am afraid of being lost to such a unity. Will my individual personality and who I am disappear in this deep, total-

---

[179] Grygiel, 17, "il cammino di coppia è un cammino fatto in due."

[180] *Ibid.*, 17, "non sta al di fuori, bensì all'interno della loro comunione sacramentale che incarna l'amore sponsale di Cristo e della Chiesa."

[181] Cf. *Reflections on Marriage, 1. At the Foundations of Personalism, b. The Order of Grace.*

gift union? I feel like I should hold something back, right? So that I am not lost?

These fears, according to St. John Paul II, are unfounded. Remember, that marriage is first a question of the person. We must keep in our sights this integral vision of the person. One need not be afraid that their individuality will be lost:

> The spiritual path of the spouses does not abstract nor skip over their (individual) personalities, on the contrary, it presupposes the *integral* person of man and woman.[182]

Husband and wife give themselves to each other in love, and this is a death to self, but in this living relationship with the Trinity, they are born anew into this unity. Their personalities are not lost but perfected.

This profound unity connects spouses on a sort of heart level. Peter can attest to this. He remembers once hearing about a group of cloistered religious sisters who would call upon the guardian angel of the sister they needed to speak to. And guess what? The sister would receive the message, and she would appear.

Imagine having that kind of connection with your spouse! This is not an appeal for some type of magical connection, but a sacramental connection of two who have been joined as one. When husband and wife

---

[182] Grygiel, 19, Emphasis added, "Il cammino spirituale dei coniugi non astrae e non salta la loro personalità, al contrario presuppone l'integrale persona dell'uomo e della donna."

strive for holiness in marriage, the Holy Spirit does not disappoint. If you open yourself, the Spirit begins to bind you in a deeper unity, almost imperceptibly and then something happens and it's like, "Woah."

When Theresa and Peter miscarried their son, Angelo Joseph (he was 18 weeks along), they went through a great deal of grief, yet life still needed to go on. Even in the cacophony of thoughts and feelings that one goes through after a sudden loss, Peter recognized Theresa's deep need. One day, as she came out to see him in the garage, before she could tell him anything, Peter hugged her and let her know he was sorry he had not given her enough affection and time as she needed. Through tears, she said she realized she had to tell him how dark her heart was feeling at the moment and so came out to say it. Before she even spoke a word, Peter had said what her heart needed to hear. That was a clear conjugal spirituality moment for them.

## Conjugal spirituality is actually the conduit that brings the truth into the reality.

Now, we understand that this may come across as heavily spiritual and that it may provoke caution not to over-spiritualize married life. Yet, even here, we look right back to that integral vision of the person being presumed. St. John Paul II was highly aware of the personalistic balance between the real and the ideal. Conjugal spirituality is the conduit that brings the truth into the reality. Conjugal spirituality does not take place only at the kneelers in the chapel but occurs during the everyday challenges of real married and family life. As Fr. Kwiatkowski notes, "The authentic vision of conjugal spirituality is only that which arises from the direct experience of love and that which occurs within it (this concrete experience of love), opening up to the spouses the perspective of holiness and sanctification."[183] When a husband lovingly gets up in the middle of the night to care for his wife when she is sick, that act of love is permeated with Christ's love. When the spouses open their hearts and lives to the grace of God, each action they do is infused with greater love and brings their union closer to God.

Conjugal spirituality is "the living relationship with the Trinity and with the spouse, in the actualization of the total delivering up of Christ for the church."[184] The vibrancy of the indwelling of the Holy Trinity within the life of the married couple makes every action they do permeated with Christ's total self-giving love. It is not merely another devotion; it is a transformation of the experiences of married life through bringing the mystery of Christ into those moments. Conjugal spirituality is the tension of the integral vision of the person played out in daily life. Who the husband and wife are is being constantly

---

[183] *Ibid.*, 20, "l'autentica visione della spiritualità coniugale è solamente quella che sorge dall'esperienza diretta dell'amore e che in essa si verifica, aprendo dinanzi ai coniugi la prospettiva di perfezione e santità."
[184] *Ibid.*, 21, "il rapport vivo con la Trinità e con il coniuge, nell'attualizzazione della consegna totale di Cristo per la Chiesa."

infused with the mystery of Christ to bring them to who they are meant to be. Conjugal spirituality is sacramental marriage lived out to the fullest. Man and wife bringing each other holiness by the action of God (grace) lived through their ordinary lives.

When Theresa is pregnant, life becomes difficult quickly. She suffers from rheumatoid arthritis and diastasis symphysis pubis, where the bones begin to pull apart unnaturally during pregnancy. It is extremely painful, and she ends up progressing from cane to walker to wheelchair by the end of a pregnancy. It's a "real" time for us, but it is a moment where Christ's love can enter into that real and through each of our own sacrifices of love and mold our hearts more towards Him. Theresa journeys through this pain with such grace, and sometimes it's tearful and sometimes she has a moment of respite above the pain, but even there, as she struggles through each hour of the day, Christ's love can enter in and transform our hearts. This also demands more on Peter when she is debilitated. He's far from perfect at this and loses his patience, but he keeps trying — to love more, to give more, to wrestle children and get them to the activities they need to be. In those efforts, Christ's love enters in. He transforms every act of love in our marriage to draw us more deeply into the heart of God, if we can open our hearts to the grace available to us.

# Does conjugal spirituality affect the sexual union of the spouses?

OK, so let's walk through what we know so far. St. John Paul II has taught us that "sacramental grace of marriage is not just some theory but a real endowment,"[185] which the spouses can use to strive toward Christian perfection. This sacramental grace affects their entire vocation and the "multilateral totality that is their conjugal life."[186] We also have learned that Christian perfection is founded in the commandment to love, and "What is love is also perfection, even when it takes place in the areas of the flesh."[187]

When St. John Paul II explained this, he was focused on the life of the married couples as a whole. However, it could also be said specifically of the sexual union between Christian spouses. Sexual intercourse is not an act that is inherently directed towards holiness in the same way that marriage is not a "state of perfection." However, because it is an act of love in the union of Christian spouses, it is possible that spouses can act in holiness in their conjugal union. As was referenced, what is love is also perfection. Christian perfection is holiness.

Made possible through the sanctifying grace of the sacrament of marriage, their conjugal spirituality elevates their sexual union to the dignity of the person. *Not to transcend it or abstract from the real corporality of*

---

[185] *Love is the Moral Foundation of Marriage, 7. The Sacramental Grace is not just a theory.*
[186] *Ibid.*
[187] *Ibid.*

*their physical union but to transform it in the physical, real experience to be an act of holy union.*

When husband and wife have oriented their lives to be open to the grace of the sacrament and are growing in their conjugal spirituality, they need not fear the flesh. Through the mystery of the Incarnation, the body has been redeemed. The fruitful communion of husband and wife is a gift from God. St. John Paul II warns us that this fear that the line is thin between sin and holiness in marriage is an "illusion."[188] There is a great difference, he notes, between those who orient themselves and their lives toward striving for Christian perfection and those that orient themselves to "spontaneous impulses."[189] Deepening one's relationship with God and with one's spouse in conjugal spirituality is an effective means of orientation toward Christian perfection.

+++

When a married couple is open to the grace of the sacrament, their marriage is the embodiment of the spousal relationship between Christ and His Church. Conjugal spirituality also makes possible the actualization of *Humanae Vitae* in the life of the spouses, which allows divine love to enter in and then leads to lasting joy.

The final point of conjugal spirituality is that you need the support of a committed community for it to grow. This is why St. John Paul II wrote The Rule for

---

[188] *Ibid.*, 6. *"Fidelity to Nature" or "Fidelity to Grace"?*
[189] *Ibid.*,

Married Couple *Groups* and not just individual couples. He recognized the need for spouses to be supported by a committed, Catholic community to give them the courage to let go and give a total gift of themselves into their marriage, every moment of every day. And in doing so, it will bring them even further into this "orbit of grace" with God.

# 15

## STUDYING MARRIAGE, APOSTOLATE, AND PRAYER
## THE RULE, #4, #5

We now look to the last three themes within the promise of the Married Couple Groups. These are the commitment to studying marriage, to serve through an apostolate, and to specific prayer.

## Studying Marriage

In the fourth point of The Rule, we see the need to constantly learn about the truth of marriage. St. John Paul II explains the primary purpose for these groups: that each couple cultivate an adequate spirituality so that "the integral teachings of Jesus Christ on marriage and family, proclaimed by the Church, could be accomplished in their married life with full understanding and full love."[190] If we want to be able to have the truth of marriage realized within our particular marriage "with full understanding," then we must continue to work to understand the teachings of the Church on marriage. This does not mean each married couple must be scholars but that they set aside time to learn the truth, even if it is only in small pieces.

If we wish to keep in mind the integral vision of the person, the real and the ideal, then we need to have a vision of what the Christian ideal for marriage truly is. We understand this Christian ideal through studying marriage. We have seen that St. John Paul II was never a micromanager; he believes in the goodness of the human heart and has great confidence that we will choose the right way. One way couples can achieve this is by incorporating a small teaching into each Married Couple Group gathering. Another idea is that the married couple be encouraged to attend an annual marriage retreat. The point is that we must continue to learn. God always has something new to teach us through Holy Scriptures and the teachings of the Church.

The reading of this book is part of that deepening of our understanding. Working to understand the rich teaching St. John Paul II has left for us (through these earlier texts and later as pope) is also part of this vision of the Christian ideal. We need to offer this beautiful vision to others as well. When we learn the

[190] *The Rule, n.4.*

joyful truth of marriage, we are inspired to reach for it.

In our professional lives, we expect a certain amount of "continuing education." If we want to get physically fit, we know that added time and effort is necessary. In the same way, if we want a strong marriage, we need to set aside time to work on our marriage. Studying marriage is a great way for us to strengthen our marriage and to deepen our spiritual life.

Studying marriage does not have to be intimidating. There are no exam questions, and you do not have to write a thesis. Even with advanced degrees in theology (specifically focused on marriage), Theresa and Peter still find that the basics shared with engaged couples when they prepare them for marriage are all that's needed to enrich their marriage.

No matter at what depth one studies marriage, there always will be a moment where you realize, "Oh yeah, we should be doing this!" That's the beauty of studying marriage—no matter what, it will offer countless opportunities for you to be a better spouse.

One thing St. John Paul II highlights in studying marriage is the need to turn our understanding of marriage to a more positive light.[191] We must affirm possibility of holiness through the love on which a marriage is founded. So, too, with the problem of contraception, the perception of the Church's teaching must be understood in a positive light. Through

---

[191] *Love is the Moral Foundation of Marriage.*

*Humanae Vitae* and the teachings of the Church on marriage, the Church is saying "Yes!" to God's great plan for love and sexuality. The Church is saying "Yes!" to a self-giving love that holds nothing back, a love that draws the spouses into the heart of God Himself.

We must give married couples the positive, joyful vision of their vocation. The demands of life will be easier to bear if they can see their vocation in light of the possibility of Christian perfection and a life of joy. We must always keep before them this beautiful ideal: who they are meant to be in the fullness of God.

All we learn in this prescription of studying marriage is only in order to deepen and *affect* our conjugal spirituality. There is a difference between being a theologian and being a Saint. Just because we learn truths doesn't mean we always put them into action. Let us commit ourselves to understand the truth in order that the truth may become real in our daily lives.

+++

# Apostolate

It is the fifth point of The Rule that sends the married couple and in fact, the group of married couples, outward in love. The apostolate should be decided upon by the group. This allows each group to develop their own charism — what is most important to them as a whole. Some groups may feel called to serve the youth ministries in their parish, while others choose to spend their apostolate assisting a pro-life ministry or serving the poor. What is important is that the group serve in this way together, thus strengthening the community between them. As a family of families, to be authentic the group's love must give and look outward.

Although Fr. Wojtyła does not list what this should be, we do find a great emphasis on the need for the entire community to be a part of the preparation of marriage. Perhaps, in a way this could be incorporated into each of the Married Couple Group apostolates. He says it is up to the whole community to prepare and support marriages in order that they might grow in Christian perfection. We must understand "the future of marriage, the future of all and each individual marriage, depends on each and every one of us."[192] The future of marriages depends on every Married Couple Group.

Aaron, a husband from a WCI Married Couple Group, reflects on the apostolate aspect of The Rule:

> I believe this is an important section in The Rule. As a Married Couple Group, we are not here just for each other but to be living witnesses to the joy that is found in the sacrament of marriage and to pour that joy back into the Church. Take time to have a discussion about what the Holy Spirit has

---

[192] *Reflections on Marriage*, 2. *Education for Marriage –the Culture of the Person.*

put on the hearts of all the couples in the group.

For our group, the apostolate we've chosen is marriage preparation and enrichment. We realized early on that all of the couples in our group, other than my wife and I, have an active role in marriage preparation through our parish. The witness from the couples in our group to invest in those preparing for marriage inspired Emily and I as well. Though we've always had an interest in marriage preparation, we often thought we were "too new" at marriage to mentor others. But, in the spirit of our Married Couple Group apostolate, we realized that we do have a lot to give as well. My wife and I are now committed to investing in younger couples — dating, engaged, or married — by inviting them over for a meal at our house to get to know them more and be a witness of the joy of marriage and parenthood for them.

+++

# Prayer

In addition to the apostolate, the group is called to prayer. Throughout our entire conversation on *how* to live an authentically Christian marriage, encountering God in prayer is vital. This is important as an individual and as a married couple (especially in order to grow in the deep unity of conjugal spirituality), but it is also important as a community. When we pray together, we support each other in a profound way — giving strength to the soul, to know you are not alone.

As we observed earlier, St. John Paul II trusted the implementation of The Rule would be accomplished in each Married Couple Group without his micromanaging. He did specify what the groups should pray for. Since it is rare that he gives such specific instructions, we should pay close attention to his words. The Married Couple Group should pray specifically for the other couples in their group, married couples in general, and for the truth of marriage and family to be understood in the Church and in the world. Each of these intentions touches on the integral vision of the person as well. The group also should pray for each specific couple; this is a prayer for the couple within their current situation (the realness of their life). They also are called to pray for all marriages. This is a more general but still "real"-focused prayer. Praying for the truth of marriage to be made known in the Church and in the world is seeing the ideal and begging God that all may see this ideal so that they may strive for it. The method of prayer a group uses is left up to the group. From more contemplative prayers to praise and worship to charismatic prayer to adoration or other manners of praying, each group will develop their own style of prayer as their group progresses and grows.

Steve and Allison, a couple from a WCI Married Couple Group, share about prayer:

As part of our weekly Married Couple
Group gatherings, we as a group not only
share our highs and lows and God
moments, but we also share our prayer
requests. By being vulnerable and sharing
these intentions with the other couples, we
grow closer to each other and become an
important part of each other's lives. Not
only are prayers being offered up for our
intentions, but as we pray for others, we
learn to grow in our own prayer life. We
can make offerings of ourselves for the
needs of others, whether it's through
prayer, fasting, abstinence, or some other
form of sacrifice. We may even find
ourselves being humbled through an
offering of ourselves for the needs of
others.

As husband and wife, we discovered that
having a dedicated prayer space in our
home has helped in our desire to pray
together as a couple. We use this space to
come together to share what's on our
hearts, to pray together, to have the Holy
Mass offered, and ultimately to grow in
our conjugal spirituality.

## St. John Paul II's witness of prayer.
### *Totus Tuus, Maria.*

St. John Paul II had a deep devotion to the Blessed
Virgin Mary. Even as a young child, he had a

connection to her. His own mother passed away when he was only nine years old. He turned to Mary during that time to be his mother in a special way. Although he wondered whether he should give his Marian devotion less emphasis, reading St. Louis de Montfort gave him the confidence to continue to lean into Mary even in his adulthood.

Cultivating a Marian devotion is also important to those following The Rule because he entrusted The Rule to Our Lady. We know this because written across the top of the handwritten pages of the first draft of The Rule are the words *Totus Tuus ego sum et omnia mea tua sunt*:

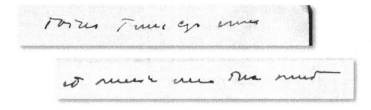

This was the saying of St. Louis de Montfort: "I am all in all to you, and all that I have is yours ... O beloved Jesus, through Mary, your holy mother." And here we find them written across the top of The Rule. We ought to offer our own marriages to Jesus through Mary as well.

St. John Paul II gave everything to Mary, even his pontificate. As soon as he was elected pope, he placed his entire pontificate under the protection of Mary. In St. Peter's Square in Rome on October 16, 1978, he said:

In this grave hour which gives rise to trepidation, we cannot do other than turn our mind with filial

devotion to the Virgin Mary, who always lives and
acts as a Mother in the mystery of Christ, and repeat
the words 'Totus tuus' (all thine)."

Then on May 13, 1981, the pontiff miraculously
survived an assassination attempt, and it was to Our
Lady of Fatima who he attributed this miracle. George
Weigel tells the story:

> John Paul would later say that 'One hand fired, and
> another guided the bullet.' It was a confession of
> miraculous intervention that the most secular soul
> might have been tempted to concede … John Paul
> II's personal answer to the question of how his
> papacy, and indeed his life, should be understood
> came in Portugal, at the shrine of Our Lady of
> Fatima, on May 12 and 13, 1982. He had gone there
> on pilgrimage on the first anniversary of Mehmet
> Ali Agca's assassination attempt, to give thanks to
> God and to Mary for his life having been spared.
> Arriving in Fatima, the Pope succinctly
> summarized his view of life, history, and his own
> mission in one pregnant phrase: 'in the designs of
> Providence there are no mere coincidences.' The
> assassination attempt itself, the fact that it took
> place on the date of the first Marian apparition at
> Fatima, the reasons it took place, his survival—
> none of this was an accident, just as the other
> incidents of his life, including his election to the
> papacy, had not been accidents.[193]

St. John Paul II shared this about his Marian
devotion in 2003:

---

[193] Weigel, 413, 440.

Jesus gives his Mother to you so that she will comfort you with her tenderness. She will discharge her ministry as a mother and train you and mold you until Christ is fully formed in you. This is why I now wish to repeat the motto of my episcopal and pontifical service: "Totus tuus" (completely yours). Throughout my life I have experienced the loving and forceful presence of the Mother of Our Lord. Mary accompanies me every day in the fulfillment of my mission as successor of Peter. Mary is the Mother of divine grace, because she is the Mother of the Author of grace. Entrust yourselves to her with complete confidence![194]

Throughout his life, he composed many prayers to the Mother of God, including this one, which is a prayer to Our Lady of Guadalupe:

O Immaculate Virgin, Mother of the true God and Mother of the Church!, who from this place reveal your clemency and your pity to all those who ask for your protection, hear the prayer that we address to you with filial trust, and present it to your Son Jesus, our sole Redeemer.

Mother of Mercy, Teacher of hidden and silent sacrifice, to you, who come to meet us sinners, we dedicate on this day all our being and all our love. We also dedicate to you our life, our work, our joys, our infirmities and our sorrows. Grant peace, justice, and prosperity to our peoples; for we entrust to your care all that we have and all that we are, our Lady and Mother.

---

[194] John Paul II, *Message of the Holy Father John Paul II for the Eighteenth World Youth Day*, March 8, 2003.

We wish to be entirely yours and to walk with you along the way of complete faithfulness to Jesus Christ in His Church; hold us always with your loving hand.

Virgin of Guadalupe, Mother of the Americas, we pray to you for all the Bishops, that they may lead the faithful along paths of intense Christian life, of love and humble service of God and souls.

Contemplate this immense harvest, and intercede with the Lord that He may instill a hunger for holiness in the whole people of God, and grant abundant vocations of priests and religious, strong in the faith and zealous dispensers of God's mysteries.

Grant to our homes the grace of loving and respecting life in its beginnings, with the same love with which you conceived in your womb the life of the Son of God. Blessed Virgin Mary, protect our families so that they may always be united, and bless the upbringing of our children.

Our hope, look upon us with compassion, teach us to go continually to Jesus and, if we fall, help us to rise again, to return to Him, by means of the confession of our faults and sins in the sacrament of penance, which gives peace to the soul.

We beg you to grant us a great love for all the holy sacraments, which are, as it were, the signs that your Son left us on earth. Thus, Most Holy Mother, with the peace of God in our conscience, with our hearts free from evil and hatred, we will be able to bring to all true joy and true peace, which come to us from your son, our Lord Jesus Christ, who with God the Father and the Holy Spirit, lives and reigns for ever and ever. Amen.[195]

When we give everything over to Mary—all our efforts, all our successes, all our failures, all of who we are—she keeps these efforts pure and keeps them above being tainted by our own sinfulness. She also helps us on our journey of faith, always guiding, loving, comforting. She is not just a Queen Mother sitting distant on a throne but wants to be your personal mother, to help you especially when you feel the realness of this "valley of tears." St. John Paul II committed The Rule and all those who follow it to Mary by writing *Totus Tuus ego sum et omnia mea tua sunt* across the top of the pages. We follow his example and place our lives in Mary's hands.

## St. John Paul II's witness of prayer
### *Divine Mercy:*
### "*There is nothing that man needs more than Divine Mercy.*"

Though not mentioned in The Rule, the devotion of Divine Mercy was dear to St. John Paul II, as was seen throughout his papacy. The first trip he took outside of Rome, after being shot, was to the Shrine of Merciful Love in Collevalenza, Italy. He said,

> A year ago I published the encyclical '*Dives in Misericordi*' ('Rich in Mercy'). This made me

---

[195] John Paul II, *Prayer to Our Lady of Guadalupe*, January 1979.

come to the Sanctuary of Merciful Love today. By my presence I wish to reconfirm, in a way, the message of that encyclical. I wish to read it again and deliver it again. Right from the beginning of my ministry in St. Peter's See in Rome, I considered this message my special task. Providence has assigned it to me in the present situation of man, the Church, and the world. It could be said that precisely this situation assigned that message to me as my task before God.[196]

When Pope John Paul II made a pilgrimage to the Shrine of Divine Mercy in Lagiewniki, Poland, on June 7, 1997, he said,

I have come here to this Shrine as a pilgrim to take part in the unending hymn in honor of Divine Mercy ... There is nothing that man needs more than Divine Mercy — that love which is benevolent, which is compassionate, which raises man above his weakness to the infinite heights of the holiness of God. In this place we become particularly aware of this. From here, in fact, went out the Message of Divine Mercy that Christ himself chose to pass on to our generation through Blessed Faustina.

And it is a message that is clear and understandable for everyone. Anyone can come here, look at this picture of the Merciful Jesus, his Heart radiating grace, and hear in the depths of his own soul what Blessed Faustina heard: "Fear nothing. I am with you always"

---

[196] St. John Paul II, homily at The Shrine of Merciful Love in Collevalenza, Italy, November 22, 1981.

(Diary, q. II). And if this person responds with a sincere heart: "Jesus, I trust in you!", he will find comfort in all his anxieties and fears. In this dialogue of abandonment, there is established between man and Christ a special bond that sets love free. And "there is no fear in love, but perfect love casts out fear" (1 Jn 4:18).

The Church rereads the Message of Mercy in order to bring with greater effectiveness to this generation at the end of the Millennium and to future generations the light of hope. Unceasingly the Church implores from God mercy for everyone. "At no time and in no historical period — especially at a moment as critical as our own — can the Church forget the prayer that is a cry for the mercy of God amid the many forms of evil which weigh upon humanity and threaten it ... The more the human conscience succumbs to secularization, loses its sense of the very meaning of the word 'mercy', moves away from God and distances itself from the mystery of mercy, the more the Church has the right and the duty to appeal to the God of mercy 'with loud cries'"(Dives in Misericordia, 15). ...

The Message of Divine Mercy has always been near and dear to me. It is as if history had inscribed it in the tragic experience of the Second World War. In those difficult years it was a particular support and an inexhaustible source of hope, not only for the people of Kraków but for the entire nation. This was also my personal experience, which

I took with me to the See of Peter and which in a sense forms the image of this Pontificate. I give thanks to Divine Providence that I have been enabled to contribute personally to the fulfilment of Christ's will, through the institution of the Feast of Divine Mercy. Here, near the relics of Blessed Faustina Kowalska, I give thanks also for the gift of her beatification. I pray unceasingly that God will have "mercy on us and the whole world" (Chaplet).[197]

And then at St. Faustina's canonization, he said:

By this act of canonization of Saint Faustina I intend today to pass this message on to the third millennium. I pass it on to all people, so that they will learn to know ever better the true face of God and the true face of their neighbor. In fact, love of God and love of one's neighbor are inseparable ... And you, St. Faustina, a gift of God to our time, a gift from the land of Poland to the whole Church, obtain for us an awareness of the depth of Divine Mercy; help us to have a living experience of it and to bear witness to it among our brothers and sisters. May your message of light and hope spread throughout the world, spurring sinners to conversion, calming rivalries and hatred, and opening individuals and nations to the

---

[197] St. John Paul II, homily at Shrine of Divine Mercy in Lagiewniki, Poland, June 7, 1997. https://www.vatican.va/content/john-paul-ii/en/travels/1997/documents/hf_jp-ii_spe_07061997_sr-faustina.html

practice of brotherhood. Today, fixing our
gaze with you on the face of the risen Christ,
let us make our own your prayer of trusting
abandonment and say with firm hope: Christ
Jesus, I trust in you![198]

We incorporate Divine Mercy into our lives, not
just as extra prayers to say but to let the mercy of God
penetrate our marriages, affect our spirituality, and
draw us together closer and closer to the heart of our
Father.

---

[198] St. John Paul II, homily at the Canonization of Sr. Mary
Faustina Kowalska, Sunday, 30 April 2000.
https://www.vatican.va/content/john-paul-
ii/en/homilies/2000/documents/hf_jp-
ii_hom_20000430_faustina.html

# 16

## LIGHTING UP THE DARKNESS
## *WITH THE SPARK OF POLAND*

So, here we are. We've come to the end of our discovery of this amazing gift from St. John Paul II that was left unwrapped for more than fifty years. We dove in deeply and soaked in his wisdom, marveled at the mystery of grace available in the sacrament of marriage, and took a second look at *Humanae Vitae*.

We pondered at how sanctified, how truly holy, our marriage vocation could be. We marveled at the thought of ourselves as the "action of God" in the life of our spouse or at how profoundly united we could be spiritually to have one interior life between us.

We contemplated whether we could see other couples in the real and the ideal, to acknowledge their struggles and earnestly listen to them yet still lovingly encourage them to holiness. We wondered whether we could be a part of a community that radically lived the Gospel, and if all of us, in that gift of self in love in our daily lives, could begin to affect cultural change together.

We see now that St. John Paul II's vision for The Rule was to empower good married couples and bring them to spiritual greatness in Christ, through sacramental grace and the support of Christian community. We may have even witnessed that lasting joy really is possible in marriage despite the chaotic, busy culture in which we live.

Knowing all this, where do we go from here?

We take what we've learned and put it into action in our lives. At the end of part 1, we spoke about the initiative to formally implement The Rule. The Wojtyła Community & Institute (WCI) is a nonprofit organization whose only mission is to help couples live out The Rule of St. John Paul II. The WCI helps couples begin a Married Couple Group following The Rule and offers a workbook, which is a phenomenal resource to guide the group week by week in prayer, education, and the essence of how the themes of The Rule play out in their marriage

The inspiring and prayerful team at the WCI also offers support through leadership training, continued education on The Rule, Leader Insights guide, community events, retreats, resources for marriage directors and pastors, and so much more.

Together we are building not only local communities radically living the Gospel but a network of communities, supporting each other and living under the guidance of St. John Paul II. The Holy Father spoke of the role of this community not only to support individual marriages but to affect a cultural change by rebuilding the culture of the person in the Church and the world. Indeed, "The future of the world and the Church passes through the family."[199]

## We must build community to overcome the challenges from modern culture.

St. John Paul II could already see in 1957 the socioeconomic changes that were transforming modern society. These changes would greatly affect the dignity of the person and the way in which marriages and families would live. He brought specific focus on the three most pivotal changes: "the necessity for both spouses to work professionally, with all its consequences on family life and children upbringing, the lack of material means necessary to start and support a family, and the most acute, especially in large cities, the lack of housing."[200]

Society is pushing spouses into a mode of existing not always compatible with raising a family in a Christian way. He calls this the "dead end" in which spouses can get stuck. These same struggles ring true even today. Many people have a feeling that there just aren't enough options for their family to grow in faith because work, school, and sports activities take up so much time. They also have to be diligent in following every child's class to make sure the faith is not being

---

[199] Familiaris Consortio, 75.
[200] *Reflections on Marriage, 3. Economy and Personalism.*

undermined. In some situations, a family may decide to homeschool; in other cases, that may not be possible.

All of the challenges coming from an increasingly anti-Christian culture, reveal a shift away from the understanding of the integral vision of the person, especially acknowledging God as the author of life and human sexuality. And St. John Paul II says, when society no longer respects the dignity of the person, then we must create our own community in which the culture of the person is upheld and in which couples can be supported in living out their marriage in an authentically Christian way. [201]

This is why the WCI was founded.

The Rule has waited long enough. It is time.

+++

We leave you with three final points to keep in mind as we answer St. John Paul II's call.

# 1. We must be willing to be heroic!

Under normal circumstances, St. John Paul II says we would not oblige the faithful to heroic virtue; however, "there are certain extraordinary conditions

---

[201] *Reflections on Marriage, 2. Education on Marriage, the Culture of the Person.*

that may demand (heroism)."[202] The way we have done marriage preparation and marriage enrichment in the past, he says, is no longer enough to push back against the lifestyle of modern society. He remarks that Christians have been surprised to see their efforts no longer succeeding as they watch the decline of morality among marriages.

If we want to be able to live fully Christian lives, we need to "intensify our efforts in the moral dimension related to the culture of the person in the life of a marriage and family."[203] We cannot shy away from this reality. We must tell engaged couples the struggle they will face and how they need God's grace for heroic virtue. Engaged couples need to understand "how much this decision will demand from them in life from a moral point of view."[204] This is not to frighten but to encourage the couple to strive for Christian perfection.

More importantly than preparing engaged couples, we need to "raise the standards for ourselves" as well.[205] We must look into our own lives and find the courage to live radically for Christ.

Do not let this discourage you. We must remember that Christianity is a conversion of oneself to the person of Jesus Christ, not only following a set of a few guidelines. You don't have to force yourself to be some kind of lone warrior. As we grow closer in our

---

[202] *Ibid.*
[203] *Ibid.*
[204] *Ibid.*
[205] *Ibid.*

relationship with Christ and our spouse, we will gain courage, hope, and vision.

With the support of a community, we can find strength to rise up and no longer feel stuck or boxed into a spiritual "dead end" nor lose sight of this total life conversion. In striving for holiness and living in the "orbit of grace" with God, a couple will be able to live their marriage in joy.

## 2. Focus on the primary purpose of The Rule: building conjugal spirituality!

The main goal in following The Rule is the spouses' holiness, including supporting each other as we grow closer to God. Even as we get excited about the different aspects of living The Rule (being social, having strong Christian friends, sharing time with other families, and serving an apostolate together), we must always remember that our united relationship to God is the goal.

The great news is that this growth in conjugal spirituality is possible because every Catholic married couple already has everything they need! We received it when we said yes to our spouse at the altar: the special grace of the sacrament of marriage. When we learn to open ourselves more fully to grace, conjugal spirituality is able to grow. The greater their openness, the more it will grow.

Conjugal spirituality, that "living relationship with the Trinity and with the spouse,"[206] helps us live in love of God and not out of mere obligation.

It is conjugal spirituality that allows God's ideal for us to break into our real, daily lives. Who the husband and wife are in their daily, ordinary life is being infused with the mystery of Christ's self-giving love for the Church in order to bring the spouses to who they are meant to be.

While every person was created to live in communion, spouses have a unique gift to profoundly and personally give yourself, body and soul, to another. And as we give ourselves away in love, we become more clearly the image and likeness of God. As Archbishop Fulton Sheen reflects:

> Love that is ever seeking to give and ever defeated by receiving is the shadow of the Trinity on earth and therefore a foretaste of heaven. Father, Mother, Child, three persons in the unity of the human nature: such is the Triune law of Love in heaven and on earth.[207]

How beautiful that a holy family reflects the love of God to the world!

A unified, total gift of self in love to the other and abandonment to the will of God is the threshold spouses must cross in order to grow their conjugal

---

[206] Grygiel, 21, "il rapport vivo con la Trinità e con il coniuge."
[207] Ven. Fulton Sheen, *Three to get Married*, (Scepters Publishers: Princeton, 1951) 66-67.

spirituality and live a marriage of lasting joy. (Do not worry. God's grace will help you!)

# 3. We must not be afraid!

Be not afraid of giving yourself away in love to your spouse and to God. This unique closeness that spouses have in their potential to reflect the Trinitarian love of God, who is a communion of divine Persons, is a fact that, St. John Paul II says, "uplifts and illuminates, but can also overwhelm and frighten."[208] Our individualities are precious to us and there could be a great fear that in giving all of ourselves to this loving union, our own uniqueness would be lost. However, let us remember that:

> The spiritual path of the spouses does not abstract nor skip over their (individual) personalities, on the contrary, it presupposes the *integral* person of man and woman.[209]

Our personalities are not lost but perfected.

The total self-gift in love to each other and to God is a dying to self; however, in this living relationship with the Blessed Trinity, we are born anew into this unity. We truly become our best selves, and it helps

---

[208] *Reflections on Marriage, 1. At the Foundation of Personalism, b. The Order of Grace.*
[209] Grygiel, 19, "Il cammino spirituale dei coniugi non astrae e non salta la loro personalità, al contrario presuppone l'integrale persona dell'uomo e della donna."

carve us into who we are meant to be. Your entire lives are immersed in the love of God. Together with your spouse you enter into an "orbit of grace" with God, which imbues your daily actions, choices, and struggles with the life and love of God. Not only will we be able to better carry our daily crosses, but we will be able to carry them with lasting joy.

And this result of lasting joy in one's life is a goal worthy of the sacrifice. When a couple can, in their unity, be drawn into this "orbit of grace," they are wrapped in divine love. And God, who is Love, renews their spousal love, perfects their individuality, enters into every fiber of their union and remakes them, drawing them into His divine life; they walk on the earth, but they live in heaven.

When divine love has kissed your marriage, there is no cross that will be too heavy to bear. The pleasures of the modern world then lose their grip upon the spouses' souls, for they pale in comparison to the rapture of union with God

In her diary, Saint Faustina recounted that Jesus promised her:

I bear a special love for Poland, and if she will be obedient to My will, I will exalt her in might and holiness. From her will come forth the spark that will prepare the world for My final coming. (n. 1732).

Many see St. John Paul II as this spark, this light from Poland. Not only was he the most influential pope in modern times, but now he has left for us — when it seems we need it most! — The Rule, which spouses can follow as a guide through these challenging times.

God is asking us to pick up the torch of this light from Poland and carry it to the world once more. This is the key to transforming the culture through the family, marriage by marriage, by supporting spouses and showing them the sanctity possible for them.

One spark can light up the darkness. Let us, together, carry the spark from Poland forward. Let us bring the light of Christ to spouses. Let us open ourselves to the Holy Spirit. Let us be courageous. Let us create a groundswell of new evangelization that washes out the influence of secularism.

A new dawn of Catholicism awaits. Together we will march forth with St. John Paul II's voice ringing in our ears, "Be not afraid!"

# JOIN A WCI MARRIED COUPLE GROUP TODAY!

1. Go to Wojtylaci.com

2. Send a message to the WCI Team. Let us know who you are, where you live, and what inspired you to reach out to us.

3. We will get back to you within 48 hours and let you know the next steps to joining (or starting) a Married Couple Group in your area and becoming the change of culture you've been longing for.

4. Or email us directly at info@wojtylaci.com. We look forward to hearing from you!


If you are a pastor or marriage director, ask us about our WCI local launch plan! We are here to serve you and bring The Rule of St. John Paul II to as many people as possible!

# ABOUT THE AUTHORS

 Peter and Theresa Martin always felt called to place their marriage at the service of the Church. The first four years of their spousal life were spent in Rome, Italy studying theology. They attended the Pontifical University of St. Thomas, the *Angelicum*, and in their fourth year, Peter began studying at the Pontifical John Paul II Institute in Rome.

After returning to the States, Peter completed his Licentiate in Sacred Theology from the Pontifical John Paul II Institute for Studies on Marriage and Family in Washington, D.C.

Theresa finished her Masters in Theology, with specificity in Marriage and Family, from the Maryvale Institute International Catholic College in Birmingham, England. St. John Paul II's *Rule for Married Couple Groups* was the primary text of her Masters dissertation.

The Martins are also published authors and were featured in the Vatican institutional journal *Educatio Catholica*.

In addition to founding the Wojtyla Community and Institute with his wife, Peter is the Director of the Office of Life, Marriage & Family as well as the Director of Communications for the Diocese of Winona-Rochester, Minnesota. Theresa is the Executive Director of the WCI; however the most important fruit of her vocation is being mother and home educator to their children, which brings her great joy.

They have been married over twenty years, laugh often, and know this is all God's doing; they are just along for the ride. To meet the Martins is to meet your next best friends; they are always ready to welcome company, share great food, have lively conversations, pray together, tell the most groan-worthy dad jokes, and pour you a glass of wine. They reside in the Wisconsin countryside along with their eight children.

# Appendix

# HISTORY OF CHURCH'S TEACHING

## *Humanae Vitae* merely reaffirmed a well-established teaching.

In proclaiming within *Humanae Vitae* that "each and every marriage act must remain open to the transmission of life,"[210] St. Paul VI was affirming teaching that was well-established within the Church dating back to the first century. To illustrate this, here are just a few of the many examples available. In the *Didache* written in 80A.D., there is a similar clash between Christianity and the ideals of the world around it: "There are two ways: one of life and one of death and great is the difference between them."[211]

---

[210] *HV*, 11.
[211] Didache, 1.

Further on it speaks more specifically to marriage and the conjugal act:

> You shall not commit adultery. You shall not seduce boys. You shall not commit fornication. You shall not steal. You shall not practice magic. You shall not use potions. You shall not procure abortion, nor destroy a newborn child.[212]

In the writings of the Church Fathers, there are numerous mentions of speaking against potions and "medicines of sterility." In reaction to a world that saw children as a burden, St. John Chrysostom speaks of "that which is sweet, and universally desirable, the having of children"[213] and St. Caesarius of Arles even says "who is he who cannot warn that no woman may take a potion [an oral contraceptive or abortifacient] so that she is unable to conceive ... chastity is the sole sterility of a Christian woman."[214] St. Augustine (354–430) also must defend the sanctity of marriage against the world. The Manicheans rejected it as evil, and the Jovinians argued that the Church demeans marriage. Augustine set forth three purposes of marriage, and the first purpose is children. This affirms St. Paul VI's preaching of the importance of openness to life. The second purpose, according to Augustine, is matrimonial loyalty, and the third is sacramental (not

---

212 *Ibid.*

213 St. Chrysostom, *Homilies on Matthew 28:5* (391 A.D.).

214 St. Caesarius of Arles, *Sermons 1:12* (522 A.D.).

in the full sense of the word sacrament but meaning that marriage was a sign of Christ and the Church).[215]

During the medieval time, contraception was condemned as an antilife act:

If anyone for the sake of fulfilling sexual desires or with premeditated hatred does something to a man or woman, or gives something to drink, so that he cannot generate or she cannot conceive or offspring be born, let him be held a murderer.[216]

St. Thomas Aquinas (1225 – 1274) also condemns contraception seeing it as a violation of natural law and, therefore, an act against the author of that law, God. He says:

Not, in fact, should it (contraception) be deemed a slight sin for a man to arrange for the emission of semen apart from the proper purpose of generating and bringing up children.[217]

Even during the Protestant Reformation, the totality of Christianity agreed on their condemnation of contraception. Martin Luther wrote, "The exceedingly foul deed of Onan, the basest of wretches ... is the most disgraceful sin. It is far more atrocious

---

[215] *Cf.* Ludwig Ott, "The Sacrament of Matrimony," *Fundamentals of Catholic Dogma*, (Tan Books Publishers, Inc.: Rockford, Illinois, 1952), 462.

[216] Quoted in William E. May, *Catholic Bioethics and the Gift of Human Life*, (Our Sunday Visitor: Huntington, IN, 2000), 144.

[217] *Ibid.*

than incest or adultery."[218] In fact, all Christian denominations were united in opposition to the use of contraception for nineteen centuries until the Anglican Church allowed its use at the 1930 Lambeth conference when it stated in Resolution 15:

> In those cases where there is such a clearly felt moral obligation to limit or avoid parenthood, and where there is a morally sound reason for avoiding complete abstinence, the Conference agrees that other methods may be used.[219]

Even in this concession, the Anglican Church also reiterated a strong statement against the use of contraception:

> The Conference records its strong condemnation of the use of any methods of conception-control for motives of selfishness, luxury, or mere convenience.[220]

However, once the "Pandora's box" of contraception was opened within culture, there was no controlling which motives prompted its use. It has been said that the "promulgation of Resolution 15 proved to be a watershed moment in the history of Ecclesiastical attitudes towards contraception."[221] After this

---

[218] Martin Luther, quoted in Provan, Charles D., *The Bible and Birth Control*, (Catholic Answers, 2018).

[219] Lambeth Conference, (1930) *Article 15*.

[220] *Ibid.*

[221] Florin Curta, Holt, Andrew, *Great Events in Religion: An Encyclopedia of Pivotal Events in Religious History*, (ABC-CLIO: Denver, 2017), 902.

pronouncement, one by one, every Protestant denomination embraced the use of contraception.

# LEARN MORE ABOUT *HUMANAE VITAE*

Atkinson, Joseph, Allan Carlson, Paul Gondreau, Mark Latkovic, Shaun and Jessica McAfee (2018), *Inseparable: Five Perspectives on Sex, Life, and Love in Defense of* Humanae Vitae, El Cajon: Catholic Answers.

Eberstadt, Mary (2012), *Adam and Eve After the Pill*, San Francisco: Ignatius Press.

Smith, Janet ed. (1993) *Why Humanae Vitae was Right: A Reader*. San Francisco: Ignatius Press.

Smith, Janet ed. (2018) *Why Humanae Vitae Is Still Right*. San Francisco: Ignatius Press.

Every WCI Married Couple Group (MCG) goes through *Humanae Vitae* during their meetings. The MCG curriculum allows groups to discuss the encyclical together. It is a wonderful opportunity to deepen the understanding and application of *Humanae Vitae* in the lives of couples. Contact the WCI (info@wojtylaci.com) or visit our website to learn how to begin a group in your area: wojtylaci.com.

Start a group today!

Live the Rule.

Save the World.

wojtylaci.com

CPSIA information can be obtained
at www.ICGtesting.com
Printed in the USA
BVHW041514020523
663428BV00004B/415